ABOUT THE AUTHOR

David Scott is the author of such Rider cookery books as THE VEGAN DIET (with Claire Golding) INDONESIAN COOKERY (with Surya Winata), PROTEIN-BALANCED VEGETARIAN COOKERY and MIDDLE EASTERN VEGETARIAN COOKERY. He is a vegetarian restaurateur in Liverpool and a martial arts enthusiast (Black Belt 4th Dan).

ALSO BY DAVID SCOTT

RECIPES FOR LIVING
THE JAPANESE COOKBOOK
GRAINS, BEANS, NUTS
MIDDLE EASTERN VEGETARIAN COOKERY
TRADITIONAL ARAB COOKERY
INDONESIAN COOKERY (with Surya Winata)
PROTEIN-BALANCED VEGETARIAN COOKERY
THE VEGAN DIET (with Claire Golding)
THE FIGHTING ARTS (with Mick Pappas)
THE INTERNATIONAL VEGETARIAN
(with Jack Santa Maria)
A TASTE OF THAILAND (with Kristiaan Inwood)

FAR EASTERN VEGETARIAN COOKERY

Over 200 distinctive recipes from China, Japan, Thailand and Indonesia

David Scott
Illustrations by Steve Hardstaff

CENTURY
LONDON   MELBOURNE   AUCKLAND   JOHANNESBURG

TX
837
.S327
1987

Copyright © David Scott 1987
Illustrations © Steve Hardstaff 1987

First published in 1987 by Century Hutchinson Ltd,
Brookmount House, 62–65 Chandos Place, Covent Garden,
London WC2N 4NW

Century Hutchinson Australia Pty Ltd,
PO Box 496, 16–22 Church Street, Hawthorn, Victoria 3122,
Australia

Century Hutchinson New Zealand Ltd,
PO Box 40–086, Glenfield, Auckland 10,
New Zealand

Century Hutchinson South Africa Pty Ltd,
PO Box 337, Bergvlei, 2012 South Africa

British Library Cataloguing in Publication Data

Scott, David, 1944–
Far Eastern vegetarian cookery: over 200 recipes from China, Japan,
Thailand and Indonesia.
1. Vegetarian cookery   2. Cookery, Oriental
I. Title
641.5′636′095   TX837

ISBN 0–7126–1430–3

Photoset by Deltatype, Ellesmere Port, Cheshire
Printed in Great Britain by
The Guernsey Press Co. Ltd,
Guernsey, Channel Islands

Contents

Introduction	7
Ingredients	11
Quantities and Menus	14
Equipment	16
Cooks' Notes and Glossary	17
Starters and Snacks	32
Stocks and Soups	47
Pickles, Salads and Dressings	59
Vegetable Dishes	79
Rice Dishes (Including Sushi)	93
Noodle Dishes	112
Egg Dishes	127
Beancurd (Tofu) and Tempe Dishes	134
Desserts	141
Conversion Tables	151
Index	153

Acknowledgement

I would like to thank Sue Bletcher of the Bluecoat Restaurant, Liverpool, for supplying many of the Chinese vegetarian recipes given in this book.

Introduction

The aim of this book is to present a series of unusual, exciting and practical Far Eastern vegetarian recipes that can be prepared straightforwardly in a Western kitchen from readily available ingredients without any special equipment or expertise.

Far Eastern Vegetarian Cookery is a sister volume to my *Middle Eastern Vegetarian Cookery* (Rider Books, 1981) and, like the cuisines of the Middle East, the cooking styles of the Far East have produced many vegetarian dishes. They have developed naturally out of the ingredients most easily available to the peasant peoples of the area (e.g. grains, soya bean products, vegetables and fruit) and through the influence of Buddhism. This religion, which encourages vegetarianism, has had considerable historical influence on both the cultural and religious life of all the countries of the Far East, although nowadays only Thailand and Japan are predominantly Buddhist in faith.

The recipes in this book have been drawn from China, Japan, Thailand and Indonesia. Chinese cooking has had some culinary influence on the other three but each of them, and particularly Japan, has its own distinctive style. I chose these four countries because together they represent the main cooking styles of the Far East. They do, however, have some common factors which give the book cohesiveness. Firstly, they use the same basic ingredients and flavourings, which are rice, noodles, soya bean products, vegetables, garlic, ginger, chilli peppers and, in Thailand and Indonesia, coconut milk, cumin, coriander and peanuts. Secondly, the main cooking methods – stir frying, deep frying, braising and steaming – are the same in each country. Finally, the way meals are presented throughout the Far East is very similar. Individual dishes are made in smaller quantities but in greater variety than in the West. They are then all served simultaneously with a central bowl of rice and accompanying pickles and sauces. The diners eat the food in whatever order and combination appeals to them. Desserts as we know them are normally reserved for snacks, and the meal is finished with a simple bowl of fruit. Chopsticks, or more recently a spoon and fork, are used to eat with, and for this reason all the food is cut into mouth-sized portions before cooking. Incidentally, this allows the food to be cooked quickly, which both saves fuel and ensures that the food retains its nutritional value – important factors in peasant economies.

Apart from these similarities the recipes selected also reflect the particular styles and favoured ingredient combinations of each of the source countries. Thai food is hot, spicy and well flavoured with fresh herbs. Indonesian dishes are also often chilli pepper hot, but because Indonesian cooking is influenced by Indian and Arabian tastes they are also both fragrant and aromatic with spices. Japanese cooks lay great store on using excellent ingredients and preparing them in a way that preserves their intrinsic flavours and textures. The main seasonings used are soya sauce, miso, garlic, sesame seeds, vinegar, root ginger, togarashi (a spice mixture not unlike black pepper) and mirin (medium sweet sherry is very similar). Chinese food, with its wonderful combinations of soft and crunchy textures and flavours of garlic, ginger, bean paste, sesame, chilli and soya sauce, is familiar to us all.

Finally, each country also brings particular national qualities to its cooking. Any discussion of these points is necessarily subjective and bound to create argument, but here is my own very brief view of the special attributes of each of the cuisines of the source countries. Indonesian cooking brings colour, presentation and flair. Thai cooking brings individuality, creativity and a strong visual sense. Japanese cuisine shows a great respect for the essential qualities of each ingredient and its relationship with other ingredients. Finally, the Chinese bring a finely tuned sense of balance and harmony to the task of uniting taste, texture, aroma and colour in multi-ingredient dishes.

Note Where the origin of a recipe is not obvious from its title or introductory note, the name of the originating country is given alongside the recipe. The very few exceptions to this rule comprise recipes that are in general use throughout the Far East.

Ingredients

Most of the ingredients required for the recipes in this book are available at any well-stocked supermarket. Those which are not are easily obtained from one of the many Oriental or Asian food stores now – fortunately for us – to be found in most of our towns and cities. In this respect I am lucky. My home town of Liverpool contains many of these stores and one in particular, called Matta's after the owner, seems literally to stock everything one needs for preparing meals originating from anywhere between London and Tokyo. As a final safeguard, for those users of the book who have no access to special ingredients, I have, where appropriate, suggested good substitutes.

Store Cupboard

The following ingredients are required in varying degrees throughout the book and it may be useful to have them in the store cupboard. The basics list gives ingredients that are used often, the extras list names ingredients that are useful to have available, and the luxury list includes items that will enhance a particular recipe and give it a taste of authenticity, but which are not essential. Any listed items with which you may be unfamiliar are described under Cook's Notes and Glossary.

Basics

vegetable oil (peanut, sesame or soya are good)

soya sauce (naturally fermented variety like Tamari)

rice

noodles

lemons or limes

chilli peppers, fresh or dried

hot pepper sauce

black peppercorns

salt

garlic

cumin seeds

coriander seeds and leaf (Chinese parsley)

root ginger

rice vinegar or cider vinegar

sesame seeds and sesame paste (tahini)

turmeric

brown sugar

Extras

miso (fermented bean paste)

peanuts or peanut butter

coconut milk (canned) or desiccated coconut

Chinese dried black mushrooms

Luxuries

bean paste and black bean sauce

togarashi (a Japanese pepper mixture; black pepper mixed with cayenne is a substitute)

mirin (similar to Chinese rice wine; medium sweet sherry is a substitute)

five-spice powder (Chinese spice mixture)

lemon grass (South East Asian plant; grated lemon rind is a substitute)

tamarind (produces a sour juice used for flavouring; lemon or lime juice are substitutes)

Japanese dried mushrooms (shiitake) or Chinese dried mushrooms

coriander root (used in some Thai dishes only)

Quantities and Menus

The recipes are in the main sufficient for four people; exceptions to this rule are indicated in the recipes concerned. The chapters are presented in a manner which allows recipes to be selected either for a Western meal which is served in different courses, or for a Far Eastern meal in which all the dishes are served at approximately the same time. To prepare a Far Eastern menu select from the recipes one or more of each of the following, depending on how elaborate the meal is to be: rice dish, soup, salad, vegetable dish and one other main dish such as a noodle, beancurd or egg recipe. Serve with accompanying small bowls of sauces and pickles. A general guide for quantities is to make one dish per guest. Thus for a party of six people you would select and prepare six recipes, including dishes from at least four different categories. Serve them at the same time and allow the diners to help themselves in whatever order and combination they choose.

Far Eastern food combines agreeably with the cuisines of other cultures and, as mentioned above, the recipes may also be used in a conventional menu as starters, soups, main courses and so on.

Note The relative quantities of ingredients given in the recipes, particularly of herbs and spices, are only guides and should be adjusted if necessary to suit the personal tastes of the cook or his or her guests.

Equipment

No special equipment is required, but the following items make some jobs simpler. A wok as opposed to a large pan or frying pan makes stir frying much easier. It may also be used for deep frying, sautéing, simmering and steaming (with a bamboo steamer). A hand or electric grinder or a large pestle and mortar are very useful for grinding herbs and spices. This is a particularly necessary task in some of the Thai and Indonesian recipes where spices, herbs and other ingredients need to be crushed into a paste with oil before cooking. For steaming, a bamboo steamer as opposed to a colander over a pan is both nicer to use and more efficient. A set of good sharp knives are not only a joy to use but will also, paradoxically, reduce the risk of a cut finger which normally results from a blunt knife slipping. A thick, unvarnished chopping board is an excellent partner to a good set of knives.

Cook's Notes and Glossary

Beancurd (Tofu in Japan, Tahu in Indonesia) and Tempe

Beancurd and tempe are both soya bean products. Beancurd is common throughout the Far East, while tempe is very much an Indonesian food. Beancurd is now generally available in the West from Chinese grocery stores and health food shops. Tempe is less readily available, but becoming better known. (For further details *see* the Beancurd chapter.)

Pressed beancurd

Pressed beancurd may be fried more easily than the tender, fresh, unpressed curd and is less likely to break up in dishes with long cooking times.

To press beancurd, lay the cakes of beancurd on a wooden chopping board. Place a few sheets of kitchen paper on top and then place a plate or flat dish over them. Weight the dish with a cup of water or a scales weight. Finally, tilt the board slightly (rest one end on an upturned saucer) and leave to drain for 1–2 hours. The beancurd is now ready to use.

Bean Paste

Brown bean paste, available flavoured with different spices and/or chillies, is prepared from lima beans fermented with flour and malt. Yellow bean paste is made from fermented soya beans. Sweet bean paste is prepared from soya beans (aduki beans in Japan).

Chillies

Many varieties of chilli peppers are grown, but for the purposes of this book chillies are the serrano or jalapeno types (2–4 in/5–10 cm long, ½ in/1 cm thick) which are most commonly available in the West. Three types are usually on sale: the green immature chilli; the red mature chilli, fresh or bottled; and the dried red variety. If you are cutting fresh chillies it is best to wear rubber gloves as they can irritate the skin. Do not rub your eyes while you have the gloves on, and wash the gloves immediately the job is finished. To reduce the fierceness of chilli peppers, remove the seeds before chopping the chillies and adding them to the dish. Alternatively, leave the chillies to soak in cold water for an hour before adding them to the dish. You can also add them whole and then remove them before serving.

Dried chillies are as hot as the fresh variety, but because they contain no volatile oils they do not burn the skin as quickly. Red and green chillies are equally hot, though there is no method of predicting the strength of a particular chilli, and even within the same batch some are hotter than others.

One teaspoon (5 ml) of hot pepper sauce used as a substitute for fresh or dried chillies is equivalent to 2 medium fresh or dried chilli peppers. Chinese-style hot pepper sauce, not the Mexican variety, has been used in the recipes in this book that contain chilli sauce.

Note Hotness is a mark of some Thai and Indonesian dishes but the degree of 'fire' is up to the individual cook. If you or your guests are unused to hot food, be very careful about the amount of chilli pepper you use. Always err on the careful side when deciding how much to put in.

Chinese Szechwan Pickled Vegetables

Use these with fresh vegetables and other ingredients, and never on their own; a small quantity will spike up the flavour of a mild dish. They are usually very salty, and when using them be careful about how much extra salt or soya sauce you add to the dish. A home-made recipe is given on p. 65.

Coconut Milk (Santan in Indonesia)

The following is extracted from *A Taste of Thailand* by David Scott and Kristiaan Inwood (Rider Books, 1986).

Coconut milk is not the liquid inside a coconut, which is called coconut water – it is the liquid pressed from grated coconut flesh diluted with water, or from dried coconut after it has been soaked in hot water or milk or a mixture of both. In Thailand coconut milk would normally be made from fresh coconut flesh. It is an important flavouring and thickening agent and is also used to make soup stocks. Strictly speaking, there are three grades of coconut milk used in cooking. The category depends on whether the milk has been obtained from unpressed (thick), once pressed (medium) or twice pressed (thin) grated coconut flesh.

South East Asian (Thailand and Indonesia included) cooking uses coconut milk in a number of recipes and especially in curries. This often puts off potential cooks in the West who immediately think it is an unavailable ingredient. This is not so. Coconut milk is easily made from the dried, unsweetened coconut flakes or desiccated coconut available in health and wholefood stores. It is also available tinned, and as a quick resort a substitute can be made from cow's milk mixed with coconut extract or essence, or by simply dissolving creamed coconut in hot water. Coconut cream, if called for, can be spooned off the top of refrigerated thick coconut milk, or as a good substitute you can use sour cream. Methods 1–4 below explain the various ways of making coconut milk. Method 1 makes authentic coconut milk and method 4 a convenient but only just fair substitute. Methods 2 and 3 are in between. Tinned coconut milk, if available, is the easiest way of obtaining a good-quality substitute to the newly made fresh coconut variety.

The recipes in this book that use coconut milk normally call for the all-purpose, medium-thickness variety. The recipes below show how to prepare this and also give variations for preparing thin or thick coconut milks.

Store coconut milk in the refrigerator, where it has the same shelf life as ordinary milk. It also freezes well (see p. 21 for details).

To prepare coconut milk

Methods 1–4 yield 12 fl oz (350 ml)

Method 1: coconut milk from fresh coconut
5 oz (150 g) grated fresh coconut *or* frozen grated coconut, defrosted
12 fl oz (350 ml) hot water

Put the coconut and water into a blender and process at low speed for 5 minutes. Line a sieve with cheesecloth or a dampened clean tea towel and pour into it the coconut mixture. Let it drain through for 5 minutes, and then press the residue with the back of a wooden spoon to extract the last of the milk. The liquid collected is the all-purpose coconut milk used in most of those recipes in the book that require coconut milk.

For thin coconut milk repeat the process using the coconut residue left in the sieve in place of the fresh coconut.

For a thick coconut milk follow the method for the all-purpose coconut milk but use 7 oz (200 g) grated fresh or frozen coconut.

Method 2: coconut milk from dried unsweetened coconut
2 oz (50 g) dried unsweetened coconut flakes *or* desiccated coconut
8 fl oz (225 ml) cow's milk
8 fl oz (225 ml) water

Put the coconut, milk and water into a pan and bring almost to the boil. Stir occasionally. Leave the mixture to cool slightly and then blend it for a minute or two. Line a sieve with cheesecloth or a dampened, clean tea towel and pour into it the contents of the blender. Let it drain through for 5 minutes, and then press the residue with the back of a wooden spoon to extract the last of the milk. The liquid collected is the all-purpose coconut milk used in most of these recipes in the book that require coconut milk.

For thin coconut milk, repeat the above process using the coconut residue left in the sieve, and use water in place of milk.

For thick coconut milk repeat the method for all-purpose coconut milk but use all milk rather than half milk and half water.

Method 3: coconut milk from creamed coconut
4 oz (100 g) creamed coconut
12 fl oz (350 ml) hot water

Blend the coconut cream in the hot water and strain the mixture through a sieve lined with muslin cloth or a dampened tea towel. This method makes medium-thickness all-purpose coconut milk.

For thicker or thinner milks use 1 oz (25 g) more or less creamed coconut.

Method 4: instant coconut milk
12 fl oz (350 ml) cow's milk
1 teaspoon coconut extract *or* essence

Stir the extract into the milk, and it's ready for use. For thick coconut milk use half single cream and half milk. For thin coconut milk use half water and half milk.

Storing coconut milk

Coconut milk freezes very well and it's a good idea to make more than you need and freeze the rest. Pour the milk into small plastic bags or containers, seal them and freeze. Defrost at room temperature, or submerge the plastic bag or container in hot water. A microwave oven could also be used.

Coconut cream from coconut milk

Put the coconut milk made by method 1 or 2 (thick milk variations) into a glass container in the refrigerator and leave it to rest for 30 minutes to 1 hour. The coconut cream will rise to the top and can be spooned off.

Coconut cream is sometimes used in curries and desserts. The amount obtained depends on the quality of the coconut or, if you have used the dried coconut method to make the coconut milk, the quality of the cow's milk used in its preparation and the oil content of the dried coconut.

Tinned coconut milk

Tinned coconut milk is generally available from Chinese or Indian grocery stores. Use the unsweetened variety, and stir it before use. The quality is as good as that of coconut milk made from dried coconut or from the so-called fresh coconuts available in the West.

Coriander

Also known as Chinese parsley and cilantro, coriander is an essential ingredient in Thai and, to a lesser extent, Indonesian and Chinese cooking. The leaves are used in flavouring and decoration, the crushed seeds in curries and other spiced dishes, and, unique to Thai cuisine, the roots, crushed to a paste with garlic and black pepper, are an ingredient in a variety of marinades and sauces.

Fresh coriander leaves are the best. If they are definitely unavailable they may be replaced for flavouring purposes by the dried herb, and for garnishes fresh parsley, basil or mint may be substituted for colour but not for flavour. Fresh coriander roots can be found on the stems of bunches of fresh coriander, although in the West the natural long, trailing roots have usually been cut short. However, by cutting off all the available roots plus a little of the stems enough roots can normally be collected to proceed with a recipe. Having said that, I am aware that a recipe requiring coriander roots may seem to a Western cook too obscure to tackle, and I have not included them in any of the recipes in this book.

Cumin

In South East Asian cooking the aromatic spice cumin is invariably used in conjunction with coriander. For the best flavour buy cumin and coriander seeds and grind them yourself before use. Cumin is also an ingredient in curry powders and pickling spices.

Curry Leaves

Obtained from a tree native to South East Asia, they are used fresh or dried in curries and powdered in curry powders. I have not included any in the recipes in this book.

Daikon

Japanese white radish (*see* Vegetables).

Daun Salem Leaves

These are used in Indonesian cookery in the same way that we use bay leaves, which may be substituted, although the flavour is not quite the same.

Dried Mushrooms

Chinese dried black mushrooms

These mushrooms have a different flavour from the mushrooms we normally use. Readily available in Chinese grocery stores, they are always sold dried and they need soaking for 30 minutes in hot water before use. The stems are tough and inedible, and need to be cut off after the soaking period.

Shiitake

These are the Japanese equivalent of Chinese dried black mushrooms. They are tree mushrooms cultivated by injecting fungus into the soft bark of water-soaked tree trunks. They are always sold dried and are reconstituted in the same way as

Chinese dried mushrooms. Generally the caps are criss-crossed with light knife cuts before cutting.

Ginger

Root ginger is used extensively in Far Eastern cooking. When buying ginger look for plump roots with a smooth, shiny, unwrinkled skin. Peel before use, and finely chop or grate for cooking. To obtain ginger juice, press the grated root in a garlic press.

Kecap

Indonesian soya sauce (*see* Soya Sauce).

Laos (Galanga)

A member of the ginger family, it has a similar flavour and is used fresh or powdered in South East Asian cookery. I have not used it in this book.

Lemon Grass

An aromatic grass native to South East Asia, it is used fresh, dried or powdered (called sereh powder) and has a lemon flavour. Grated lemon rind may be substituted, and this is what I have done in the recipes that in the original included lemon grass.

Loh Baak

Chinese white radish (*see* Vegetables).

Mirin

A Japanese rice wine used only for cooking. Medium sweet sherry may be substituted.

Miso

Miso is fermented soya bean paste. Naturally fermented miso will keep indefinitely, and the flavour improves with age. It is rich in protein and vitamins and forms a basic part of the diet of many countries in the Far East, particularly Japan. Combined with rice or other grains, it supplies all the essential amino acids, and it is a good source of vitamin B12, which is often lacking in a strict vegetarian diet. If carefully fermented, it also contains enzymes to aid the digestion. Miso is traditionally fermented for 4–5 days, and then aged for 2 years or more.

The taste of the finished product depends on many factors, and no two miso taste exactly the same. Of the miso pastes available in the West, there are three main varieties. Mugi miso is the commonest and most popular. Made from 50 per cent barley and 50 per cent soya beans, it is an all-purpose miso, medium brown in colour. Hacho miso is aged for longer than mugi, and contains more salt. It is stronger in flavour and darker in colour. Used more often in the winter months, hacho miso wards off the cold. Kome miso is lighter and more delicately flavoured than the other two. It is used in the preparation of dishes that require more subtle flavours.

Miso is a remarkably versatile ingredient. It may be used as a base for soups or sauces, in a marinade for vegetables, as a dressing with vinegar or lemon for salads, or in the stock for casseroles or stews.

Nori

A purple seaweed sold in paper-thin sheets 8 in (20 cm) square, it is available in Japanese grocery stores in packets of 10 sheets. Nori is used extensively in Japanese cooking for seasoning, garnishing and wrapping other foods (*see* Sushi Rice Dishes in the Rice Dishes chapter).

Onions

A number of the recipes require spring onions (known as scallions in the United States) either in the cooking or as a garnish. Regular, finely chopped onions used in the same quantities may be substituted in the cooking if spring onions are unavailable. Chives make a good substitute as a garnish.

The recipes here have been tested using common white or brown onions, but shallots are slightly closer in taste to the onions generally used in Far Eastern cooking. If shallots are available and you wish to use them in the recipes, substitute 4 oz (100 g) shallots for 1 medium onion.

Peanuts

Dry roasted and crushed, peanuts are widely used in Thai and Indonesian cookery. An equal weight of peanut butter may be substituted.

Sambal

A hot or spicy sauce or relish. Sambals are served in a number of varieties in small bowls as accompaniments to an Indonesian meal.

Santan

Indonesian coconut milk (*see* Coconut Milk).

Sesame

Sesame seeds, lightly dry roasted and used whole or crushed, are a common ingredient in Japanese and Chinese cookery. Sesame paste is available in jars in Chinese grocery stores, or from wholefood shops as tahini. Sesame seeds mixed with salt form a Japanese condiment called gomashio.

Shiitake

Japanese dried mushrooms (*see* Dried Mushrooms).

Shoyu

Japanese soya sauce (*see* Soya Sauce).

Snow Fungus

A white, odourless and tasteless fungus, it is soaked in water before use, when it expands a lot and becomes soft and gelatinous. Snow fungus is used in soups and in other dishes in which its delicate texture may be appreciated. It is very expensive, and therefore used sparingly.

Soba

Japanese thick buckwheat noodles.

Somen

Japanese thin wheatflour noodles.

Soya Sauce (Shoyu in Japan, Kecap in Indonesia)

Soya sauce is familiar to all Chinese restaurant patrons, although unfortunately the liquid normally found in bottles under this name is a chemically flavoured product that bears little relationship to the real thing. True soya sauce is made from a mixture of soya beans, wheat (or barley) and salt, fermented together for up to 2 years. The resultant mash is pressed and filtered, and the liquid extracted is heated rapidly to seal in the flavour and stop further fermentation. When you shop for soya sauce, make sure you buy one of the fermented varieties. Be careful not to add too much salt as well, since soya sauce is itself salty.

Kecap manis is a distinctive Indonesian soya sauce – thick, black and sweet. To make your own, dissolve 2 oz (50 g) brown sugar in 6 fl oz (175 ml) dark soya sauce. Children enjoy it sprinkled over boiled rice.

Szechwan Pepper

Moderately hot peppercorns with black seeds, they are sold whole or ground and have a smell not unlike that of coriander seeds.

Tahu

Indonesian beancurd (*see* Beancurd).

Tamarind

The tamarind tree produces a sour fruit pod, the sour juices of which are used as a flavouring agent in some Thai and Indonesian recipes (although I have often given lemon or lime juice as a substitute). The pods are sold pressed into a pulp which is soaked in water and then filtered through a sieve. The brown liquid collected, called tamarind water, is used in curries, soups, stews, sauces etc.

An easy way to prepare tamarind water in the West is to use the tamarind concentrate available from Indian grocery stores. The concentrate is diluted as required (1 teaspoon/5 ml to 3 tablespoons/45 ml water). Alternatively, lemon juice or lime juice sweetened with a little dark brown sugar may be used as a substitute. In the recipes given here tamarind water and lemon or lime juice are used in the same proportions if the latter are used as substitutes.

Tempe

See Beancurd.

Tofu

Japanese beancurd (*see* Beancurd).

Togarashi

A Japanese condiment, it is a blend of several spices which when combined taste like a cross between black pepper and cayenne.

Vegetables

The countries of the Far East use many vegetables with which we are familiar, but there are a few in common use, included in some recipes here, that are not so well known in the West. Here are some brief details of those used in this book. They are usually readily available from Asian or Oriental grocery stores.

Chinese greens

Under this heading come three varieties of Chinese cabbage.
  1. *Chinese White Cabbage (baak choi)*. Baak choi are available in a number of forms, but they are all identified by their creamy white leaf stalks. Locally grown varieties are available in summer and autumn. The smaller plants are the most tender. Both the leaves and stalk are used in soups, salads and stir fried dishes. To prepare, separate the leaves, wash well and chop as required.
  2. *Chinese Leaves (Peking cabbage)*. Two types are available, long, narrow and barrel-shaped, or short and stout. They both have crinkly, creamy yellow leaves and broad-ribbed leaf stalks. The longer variety tend to have the best flavour, at least of those available in Britain. Peking cabbage is usually in the shops from mid-autumn to late winter. To prepare it, wash well and chop as desired. It may be boiled, stir fried, braised or blanched, and used to wrap up various stuffings.

3. *Chinese Flowering Cabbage (choi sum).* Choi sum has much thinner stems than the two cabbages above, and greener leaves. It has a mild flavour and cooks quickly and uniformly. It is available most of the year round. To prepare, wash, drain and cook whole or chopped as desired. Cook very lightly by boiling, steaming or stir frying.

Bamboo shoots, water chestnuts and lotus roots

Although these vegetables are quite common in Far Eastern recipes they are generally unavailable fresh in the West. For this reason I have included them in only a few recipes, and then only when the cooked tinned varieties make an acceptable substitute for the fresh vegetable. Generally they may be used straight from the tin, after rinsing, in salads, for stir frying, deep frying, sautéing, or in soups and stews. Each of the vegetables has a crunchy texture and slightly sweet and individual flavour. They are very good for giving a contrast in texture when cooked with softer vegetables.

Beansprouts

Dried beans, particularly soya and mung beans, are sprouted to give tasty white shoots. These beansprouts have become well known and are easily available in the West. Nearly all the beansprouts seen in the shops are grown from mung beans. They are available all the year round and they make an excellent, fresh and crisp addition to salads, especially in the winter when other vegetables are in short supply. To prepare simply wash well and drain. Use fresh or stir fried.

Mushrooms

See Dried mushrooms.

White radish (daikon in Japan, loh baak in China)

White radish can be between 6 in (15 cm) and 1 ft (30 cm) or even more in length. Despite its looks, however, it is from the same family as the familiar small, red salad radish and it has a definite radish flavour. White radish is excellent raw in slices or grated in salads. It also pickles well. It is good in soups and stews and may also be boiled, stir fried or braised. To prepare, lightly peel and chop or grate as desired.

Vinegar

Rice wine vinegar or cider vinegar are the best kinds to use in the recipes in this book that require vinegar. Vinegar reacts with most metals, especially aluminium. Don't use an aluminium pan in recipes that call for vinegar, and avoid stirring such dishes with a metal implement.

Wasabi

Japanese green mustard. It is hot in flavour like English mustard, which may be used as a substitute.

Starters and Snacks

In this collection of Far Eastern starters I have tried to combine the qualities of the various cuisines of the area to produce dishes that please both the eye and the palate. As the title of the chapter implies, the recipes are very suitable as starters for a Western-style meal, but they are also designed to be served as part of a multi-dish Far Eastern dinner. Another idea is to make a selection of five or six starters and serve them as the basis of a buffet party. There are hot, cold and salad dishes to choose from, plus one or two titbits to tempt the not so hungry.

Because starters are served on their own in small amounts the ingredients should be of good appearance, colour and texture. Always choose fresh, fine-quality vegetables, fruit, grains etc. The recipes given here, particularly those from Japan, also have a certain simplicity, and it is best to serve them in bowls and plates that reflect this simplicity. Plain white china and wooden chopsticks are most in harmony.

Deep Fried Noodle Wrapped Water Chestnuts

Spicy Lemon Cucumber Salad

Chakin Sushi

Celery and Green Pepper with Sesame Sauce

Stuffed Chinese Mushrooms with Sherry Sauce

Mushroom and Vegetable Salad in Lemon Shells

Son-in-Law Eggs

Plump Horses

Green Apples with Sweet Hot Sauce

Galloping Horses

Chinese Egg Rolls

Egg Roll Skins

Dry Roasted Peanuts

Fried Peanuts

Fried Peanuts with Garlic and Onion

Crisp Sweet Walnuts or Cashews

Corn Fritters

Pan Roasted Coconut with Peanuts

Oven Roasted Coconut with Peanuts

Lotus Seed Bao

Black Bean and Walnut Sesame Bao

Vegetable Bao

Deep Fried Noodle Wrapped Water Chestnuts *Serves 4*

The coating used for this Chinese recipe is chopped fine cellophane noodles (made from mung bean flour), but other coatings may be used and you could even serve the chestnuts with two or three different ones.

5 oz (150 g) plain flour
1 egg
2 fl oz (50 ml) water
1 small can water chestnuts
4 oz (100 g) cellophane noodles
  or fine vermicelli

vegetable oil for deep frying
2 tablespoons cornflour
for dipping
soya sauce
salt
hot pepper sauce

Sift the flour into a mixing bowl and mix in the egg. Add the water and beat to a smooth batter. Set to stand for 20 minutes. Drain the chestnuts and dry each of them on an absorbent paper towel. Break the noodles into small ¼ in (0.75 cm) pieces. Heat the oil ready for deep frying. Roll each chestnut in the cornflour, then dip it into the batter and finally roll it in the broken noodles. Deep fry in the hot oil until golden brown. Drain, and serve with small dishes of soya sauce, salt and hot pepper sauce for dipping.

Variations
Other coatings that may be used are: toasted sesame seeds, chopped walnuts or almonds, or crumbled toasted nori seaweed.

Spicy Lemon Cucumber Salad *Serves 4*

This South East Asian cucumber salad is excellent both as a light, refreshing starter and as a side dish or garnish for main meals, particularly curried dishes. In the Far East it would be made from the gherkin-type cucumbers sometimes available in the West from Indian grocery stores, and used unpeeled and unseeded. Normal cucumbers are fine but must be peeled and seeded.

- 2 lb (900 g) small gherkin cucmbers, finely sliced *or* 2 medium cucumbers, peeled, seeded and finely sliced
- 1 medium onion, finely sliced
- 1 tablespoon salt
- 3 tablespoons (45 ml) lemon juice
- ¼ teaspoon cayenne pepper (add more if you like hot food)
- 2 tablespoons sesame seeds or 1 tablespoon (15 ml) sesame seed oil *or* peanut oil *or* sunflower seed oil

Combine the cucumber, onion and salt in a bowl and mix well together. Set aside for an hour and then drain off all the liquid that has formed. Gently press the cucumber and onion to extract more liquid, and discard this also. Stir in the lemon juice and cayenne. Dry roast the sesame seeds until they start to jump in the pan, then add them to the bowl together with the sesame oil. Mix well, cover, chill and serve.

Chakin Sushi *Serves 4*

Sushi is a word used to describe a variety of Japanese dishes in which cooked rice seasoned with vinegar and sugar is the basic ingredient (*see* Rice Dishes chapter). In chakin sushi, paper-thin omelettes are used to wrap the sushi rice into pouches. The edges of the pouches are secured with fine coloured string or cotton, and then topped with a garnish of cooked shrimps and green peas. They make very pretty and unusual starters.

sushi rice

12 oz (350 g) white short grain rice
1 pint (550 ml) water
4 tablespoons (60 ml) cider vinegar *or* rice wine vinegar

3 tablespoons white sugar
½ teaspoon salt

paper-thin omelettes

4 medium eggs
¼ teaspoon salt

vegetable oil

garnish

4 oz (100 g) cooked button mushrooms
2 oz (50 g) cooked green peas

1 tablespoon finely chopped parsley

Wash the rice well by stirring it vigorously in lots of water. Let the rice settle and carefully pour off all the milky residue. Repeat the process until the water remains almost clear (this will be a quick process with good-quality rice; it will take longer with loose-packed rice).

Drain the rice and place it in a heavy pan. Add the water, cover the pan and bring to the boil quickly. Turn the heat right down and allow it to simmer for 15 minutes. Turn off the heat and allow the rice to stand for 5–10 minutes. Turn the rice into a non-metallic mixing bowl and set aside.

Combine the vinegar, sugar and salt and bring the mixture to the boil. Pour this dressing over the hot rice. Stir the rice gently with a wet wooden spoon, while with your other hand fanning the rice with a flat pan lid or rolled up newspaper. This cools the rice quickly and gives it an authentic shine. Set the rice aside.

To prepare the paper-thin omelettes, beat the eggs with the salt in a mixing bowl. Very lightly coat the bottom of a heavy 8–9 in (20–22.5 cm) frying pan with oil and heat until a drop of water evaporates very quickly off the surface. Pour in one-eighth of the egg and tilt the pan to spread the egg evenly and thinly. Cook over a medium heat and turn the omelette over when the top side starts to firm up. Cook the other side for only another few seconds and then slide the omelette onto a large plate. Regrease the pan and repeat to make a total of 8 omelettes.

To assemble the chakin sushi, mould about one-eighth of the sushi rice into a lightly packed, slightly flattened ball. Place this in the middle of one of the omelettes. Gather the edges of the omelette together and draw them to the centre. Fold back the edges, leaving an opening at the top. Tie the pouch into shape by fastening fine coloured string or cotton under the folds (traditionally a thin ribbon of toasted nori seaweed is used – it is available from Japanese grocery stores).

Garnish the top of the rice in each pouch with a few mushrooms, peas and a sprinkling of parsley.

Serve two chakin sushi on each plate. Eat using chopsticks and, if necessary, the help of your fingers. You may like to provide a sharp knife for those guests who wish to cut open their egg pouches.

Celery and Green Pepper with Sesame Sauce   Serves 4

This is a light, tasty Chinese appetizer which looks delicious.

- 2–3 sticks celery, including leaves, washed
- 1 large green pepper
- 2 tablespoons (30 ml) soya sauce
- 1 tablespoon (15 ml) sesame seed oil
- 1 teaspoon brown sugar

garnish
- 8 very thin slivers fresh root ginger
- 2 teaspoons sesame seeds, dry roasted

Cut the celery diagonally into 2 in (5 cm) lengths. Retain the leaves. Cut the pepper in half, core and seed, cut in half again and then cut each piece into quarters. Heat a pan of slightly salted water to boiling and blanch the celery and pepper pieces for 30 seconds only. Remove and drain. Mix together the soya sauce, sesame oil and brown sugar. Stir this sauce into the vegetables and distribute them among 4 individual plates. Garnish each with a few chopped celery leaves, slivers of ginger root and sesame seeds.

Variation
For a sweet-sour sauce add 1 tablespoon (15 ml) lemon juice to the sauce ingredients.

Stuffed Chinese Mushrooms with Sherry Sauce   Serves 4

Black dehydrated Chinese mushrooms have large caps and are perfect for stuffing. This recipe also requires bamboo shoots. Buy a very small tin and store unused shoots under clear water. Use them within 3 or 4 days. The stuffed mushrooms are served garnished with fresh coriander leaves, sometimes known as Chinese parsley. They give the dish a characteristic flavour, but if unavailable parsley may be substituted.

8 Chinese black mushrooms
5 oz (150 g) par-cooked rice
1 tablespoon finely chopped bamboo shoots
1 spring onion, finely chopped
2 tablespoons (30 ml) soya sauce
2 teaspoons (10 ml) medium sweet sherry

2 tablespoons (30 ml) peanut oil
2 tablespoons (30 ml) stock *or* water
1 teaspoon cornflour
¼ teaspoon salt
garnish
coriander leaves, finely chopped

Cover the mushrooms in warm water and leave to soak for 30 minutes. Drain well and discard the hard, inedible stalks. Combine the rice, bamboo shoots, spring onion, half the soya sauce and half the sherry. Stir this mixture into a paste and fill each of the mushroom caps with it. Put the caps in a steamer (or between 2 plates standing on a bowl in a pan with water in the bottom) and steam for 20 minutes. Just before they are finished put the oil, stock, cornflour, salt and remaining soya sauce and sherry in a small pan and heat, stirring, until just boiling. Serve the mushrooms with the hot sauce poured over and garnished with coriander leaves.

Mushroom and Vegetable Salad in Lemon Shells   Serves 4

This Japanese-inspired starter traditionally uses white radish (daikon) but the little white turnips available in Britain in the winter and spring months are just as good. The salad is served piled high in lemon shells and looks very attractive.

2 large lemons, cut in half
4 oz (100 g) little white turnips
   or white radish, grated
4 oz (100 g) young carrots,
   scrubbed and grated
4 oz (100 g) button
   mushrooms, chopped and
   sautéed in a little oil

2 tablespoons (30 ml) cider
   vinegar
2 teaspoons sugar
½ teaspoon salt
4 sprigs parsley

Cut around the flesh of the lemons just inside the skins and scoop out the flesh, leaving 4 empty lemon shells. Squeeze the flesh and reserve the juice. Combine the turnips, carrots, mushrooms, vinegar, sugar and salt and 1 tablespoon (15 ml) of the lemon juice. Mix them well together. Divide the salad among the 4 lemon shells. Serve in attractive bowls, sprinkle a few drops of lemon juice over the salads, and garnish the tops with parsley sprigs.

Son-in-Law Eggs   Serves 4

The story behind the name of this Thai recipe is that a prospective son-in-law wanted to impress his future mother-in-law with his culinary prowess. He devised this recipe from the only dish he could make – boiled eggs. It's delicious and I'm sure he won her over, at least for a while.

oil for deep frying
4 eggs, hardboiled, shelled and
   cut in half crosswise
2 tablespoons brown sugar
2 tablespoons (30 ml) soya
   sauce
2 tablespoons (30 ml) lemon
   juice or tamarind water

garnish
2 tablespoons diced onion,
   fried brown in a little oil
2 tablespoons finely chopped
   coriander leaves
1–2 red chillies, seeded and
   thinly sliced

Heat the oil in a wok or deep frying pan with a basket until it is just beginning to smoke, and then carefully lower in the hard-boiled egg halves. Deep fry them for 3–4 minutes. Remove them and set aside to drain. Heat 1 tablespoon (15 ml) of oil in a saucepan and stir in the brown sugar, soya sauce and lemon juice. Stir and simmer over a very low heat for 5 minutes. Add the eggs and stir them very gently over the heat for 2–3 minutes. With a slotted spoon transfer the eggs to a serving plate. Garnish them with fried onion, coriander leaves and rings of chilli.

Plump Horses   Serves 4

I think the name of this Thai dish must relate to the poached egg shape of the individual portions. Anyway, it's a good talking point for the guests while they enjoy the taste.

4 eggs, beaten
4 oz (100 g) mushrooms, finely sliced and sautéed in a little oil
8 fl oz (225 ml) stock
2 cloves garlic, crushed
1 teaspoon coriander seeds, ground
1–2 spring onions, finely chopped
salt and freshly ground black pepper to taste
garnish
coriander leaves *or* mint *or* parsley, finely chopped

Combine all the main ingredients and mix well. Distribute the mixture among 4 (or 8 if they are not large enough) individual poached egg moulds. Set them in the pan with the water 1 in (2.5 cm) or so up the sides of the moulds. Cover and cook over a low heat until they are set (about 20 minutes). Serve them hot, still in the moulds, garnished with finely chopped herbs.

Green Apples with Sweet Hot Sauce   Serves 4

In Thailand this dish would be made with green mangoes, and if they are available substitute them for apples in the recipe. Otherwise use crisp, only slightly sweet apples, such as Granny Smiths. Serving apples in this way usually causes a surprise – people are not used to seeing them in such strange company.

4 crisp green apples, cored and sliced into 6
1 teaspoon (5 ml) lemon juice
3 tablespoons (45 ml) soya sauce
4 oz (100 g) white sugar
¼–½ teaspoon (1.25–2.5 ml) chilli sauce
1 tablespoon finely diced onion

Place the apples in a bowl of water to which the lemon juice has been added and put them in the fridge to chill slightly (15–30 minutes). Put the soya sauce and sugar in a small pan and gently melt the sugar in the liquid. Pour the mixture into a small bowl and set it aside for 10 minutes to cool. Now stir in the chilli sauce and onion. Set the bowl of sauce in the centre of the plate, arrange the apple slices around it, and serve.

Galloping Horses
Serves 6–8

I'm not sure why this well-known Thai dish is called Galloping Horses, but its name inspires the imagination to try it. Fresh pineapple is required in the recipe, but if it is unavailable see the variation below which uses oranges instead.

3 tablespoons (45 ml) vegetable oil (peanut oil is good)
3 tablespoons finely diced onion
1 lb (450 g) cooked rice
1 teaspoon salt
½ teaspoon freshly ground black pepper
1 tablespoon sugar
2 oz (50 g) roasted peanuts (unsalted), coarsely crushed *or* 2 tablespoons (30 ml) crunchy peanut butter
1 medium to large fresh pineapple, peeled, sliced and cored

garnish
1 red chilli, seeded and finely chopped
fresh coriander leaves *or* mint, finely chopped

Heat the oil in the frying pan and sauté the onion for 2–3 minutes or until softened. Add the onions to the rice, salt, sugar and black pepper, mix well and then stir into the mixture the crushed peanuts. Arrange the pineapple slices on individual plates and spoon a portion of the rice mixture into each. Garnish with a few rings of chilli pepper and a sprinkling of coriander or mint leaves.

Variation
Arrange the segments of 1 or 2 large oranges on lettuce leaves on individual plates. Spoon the rice mixture over, garnish as above and serve.

Chinese Egg Rolls
Makes 14

14 egg roll skins (*see* recipe below *or* buy ready-made)
5 oz (150 g) beansprouts
3 tablespoons (45 ml) vegetable oil
8 oz (225 g) celery, diced
4 oz (100 g) carrot, grated
2 teaspoons finely grated root ginger
6 spring onions, finely chopped
3 oz (75 g) bamboo shoots, shredded
8 water chestnuts, thinly sliced
good pinch salt
½ tablespoon (7.5 ml) soya sauce
½ tablespoon (7.5 ml) medium sweet sherry
1 egg, lightly beaten
vegetable oil for deep frying

Prepare the egg roll skins according to the recipe. Rinse the beansprouts and drain. Heat 2 tablespoons (30 ml) of the vegetable oil in a pan, add the celery and carrot and stir fry for 1 minute. Add the ginger, spring onions, bamboo shoots and water chestnuts. Stir fry for 1½ minutes more, then add the beansprouts and cook for a further 45 seconds. Add the salt, soya sauce and sherry and heat through. Remove from the heat, put in a colander, drain and cool completely.

Divide the mixture into 14. Place one portion slightly off the centre of each skin. Roll the skin to enclose the filling. Tuck in the sides neatly. Brush the opposite sides of the seam with the beaten egg and press together. Repeat for all the filling and skins. Place the rolls on a plate with the sealed edge down. Fry them in deep oil for 3–4 minutes. Turn the rolls once to brown evenly on all sides. Drain and serve hot.

Egg Roll Skins

Makes 14 skins

1 lb (450 g) plain flour
½ teaspoon salt
2 eggs, lightly beaten

15 fl oz (450 ml) water
2 tablespoons (30 ml) vegetable oil

Sift the flour and salt into a bowl. Make a well in the centre and add the eggs. Stir until well blended. Add the water gradually, beating with a wire whisk until the batter is quite smooth. Pour 1 tablespoon (15 ml) oil into a heavy frying pan. Heat until the oil is hot. Tip out excess oil, leaving a thin film in the pan. Pour about 2 tablespoons (30 ml) of batter into the oiled pan, tilting the pan in all directions to spread the batter evenly. Cook, on one side only, over a low heat for about 1½ minutes, until firm but not brown. Stack the pancakes on a plate and cover with a damp cloth to prevent them drying out. Brush the pan with oil before cooking each pancake. Allow them to cool completely before filling.

Dry Roasted Peanuts

Roasted peanuts, as well as being eaten as a snack, are also used as an ingredient in a number of Indonesian and Thai recipes. To roast them, simply put the raw but unskinned peanuts into a heavy, ungreased frying pan and cook them slowly, stirring constantly, over a low heat. The peanuts will give off a distinctive aroma when ready and the skins will darken in colour. Transfer them from the pan to a bowl and add salt to taste if you wish. Alternatively you can store them in an airtight container for 2–3 weeks.

Fried Peanuts *Makes 8 oz (225 g)*

These are delicious as a snack with drinks or as an accompaniment to a main meal. Stored in an airtight container, they will keep for several weeks.

8 oz (225 g) unsalted raw peanuts (buy the skinned variety *or* follow the skinning procedure given in the recipe below)

salt to taste
vegetable oil for deep frying

Heat the oil in a small but deep frying pan. Put half the peanuts into a sieve that will fit the pan. Fry the peanuts over a moderate heat, stirring, for 3–5 minutes until they are golden brown. Lift the sieve containing the peanuts out of the pan and let them drain over a bowl for a few minutes. Return the drained oil to the pan and repeat the process with the remaining peanuts. Roll the fried peanuts in absorbent kitchen paper to remove excess oil. Transfer them to a dry bowl, lightly salt them, shake well and allow to cool.

Variation
Fried Peanuts with Garlic and Onion
Serve as a snack or a side dish. Unused peanuts can be stored in an airtight container for 2–3 weeks.

1 lb (450 g) unsalted raw peanuts (buy the skinned variety *or* follow the procedure given at the beginning of the recipe)

6 oz (175 g) vegetable oil
4 cloves garlic, chopped
2 medium onions, halved and finely sliced
salt to taste

Put the unskinned peanuts in a bowl and just cover them with boiling water. Leave them to stand for 30 minutes and then skin them by rubbing the nuts individually between thumb and finger. Line a colander with absorbent kitchen paper and put the skinned nuts into it to dry.
  Heat the oil in a deep frying pan and add half the nuts. Fry them, stirring, over a moderate heat for 4 minutes or until nicely

browned. Lift the peanuts out with a perforated spoon and allow them to drain through a fine sieve. Return the drained oil to the pan and repeat the process with the remaining peanuts. Fry the garlic and onion slices in the same oil until brown and crisp. Drain them through a fine sieve. Combine the peanuts, garlic and onion slices and lightly salt the mixture.

Crisp Sweet Walnuts or Cashews *Serves 4*

China

4 oz (100 g) walnuts *or* cashews
4 tablespoons (60 ml) water
4 tablespoons sugar
oil for deep frying

Put the nuts, water and sugar into a small saucepan and bring to the boil. Simmer for 5 minutes over a low heat, then remove from the heat and marinate the nuts in the syrup for 4 hours. Turn from time to time to ensure that they are all well coated. Bring the oil to a very high heat. Then reduce the heat and, over a low flame, deep fry the nuts for about 4 minutes or until golden brown. Lift out, drain and put on a plate to cool. Serve cold.

Corn Fritters

Serve this Indonesian dish as a snack or as an accompaniment to other dishes. The corn can be replaced by the same weight of roasted peanuts. Stored in an airtight container, the fritters will keep for about a week.

6 oz (175 g) plain flour
2 oz (50 g) rice flour
½ teaspoon salt
½ teaspoon chilli powder
1 teaspoon ground coriander
½ teaspoon ground cumin
4 fl oz (100 ml) water
1 egg
1 clove garlic, crushed
1 small onion, diced
10 oz (275 g) fresh *or* tinned sweetcorn
vegetable oil for deep frying

Put the plain flour, rice flour, salt, chilli, coriander, cumin, water, egg and garlic into a blender or food processor and blend to a smooth batter. Alternatively, use a mixing bowl and whisk. Transfer the batter to a bowl and mix in the onion and sweetcorn. Put enough oil in a frying pan to give a depth of ⅓ in (½ cm) and heat it over a medium flame. Drop in 2 tablespoons (30 ml) of the batter and spread it evenly to form approximately a 4 in (10 cm) circle. Fry the fritter crisp and brown on the underside and then turn it over and brown the other side. Drain the cooked fritters on absorbent kitchen paper draped over a wire rack. Repeat for all the batter.

Pan Roasted Coconut with Peanuts

This Indonesian dish, called serundeng, can be served as a side dish or as a garnish sprinkled over vegetables. It will keep well for 2–3 weeks in an airtight container.

3 tablespoons (45 ml) peanut oil *or* other good vegetable oil
1 medium onion, finely diced
2 cloves garlic, crushed
½ teaspoon ground cumin
2 teaspoons ground coriander
6 oz (175 g) desiccated coconut
2 teaspoons dark brown sugar
juice of 2 lemons
salt and pepper to taste
6 fl oz (175 ml) water
4 oz (100 g) roasted *or* deep fried peanuts (see recipes above)

Heat the oil in a frying pan and add the onion, garlic, cumin and coriander and mix well. Stir fry the mixture for 1–2 minutes over a moderate heat. Stir into it the coconut, sugar, lemon juice and salt and pepper. Stir fry the mixture for 2–3 minutes and then add the water. Continue stirring until all the water is absorbed, then cover the pan, set to simmer and leave for 45 minutes, stirring occasionally, until the coconut is nicely browned. Remove the pan from the heat and stir in the peanuts. Allow the serundeng to cool. Serve whatever amount is needed and store the rest.

Variation
Oven Roasted Coconut with Peanuts
The ingredients are the same as for the recipe above, with the addition of 2 tablespoons (30 ml) vegetable oil. Preheat the oven to 350°F (180°C, gas mark 4). Follow the recipe above to the point where the water has just been added. Now transfer the contents of the pan to an ovenproof dish and pour over the top the extra 2 tablespoons (30 ml) of oil. Cover, and bake for 35–40 minutes. Stir now and again to prevent sticking and burning. Remove the dish from the oven and stir in the peanuts. Allow the mixture to cool, and then serve it or store it in an airtight container.

Bao (Steamed Filled Buns) — Makes 14

China

The Chinese are fond of appetizers, and all sorts of dried nuts and seeds are used. The range of snacks is infinite: anything that can be eaten separately from a main meal can constitute a snack in Chinese terms. Dim sum are snacks, and so are the many different types of sweet cakes and buns which are special to each region. Variations of these steamed buns with different fillings appear in nearly every region in China. Eaten hot or cold, they are substitutes for our sandwiches, and are often eaten on picnics.

Lotus Seed Bao — Makes 14

bao buns

1 teaspoon sugar
6 fl oz (175 ml) warm water
2 teaspoons dried yeast

filling

1 lb (450 g) can lotus seed paste
10 oz (275 g) strong white flour
½ oz (15 g) butter

Mix the sugar, warm water and yeast together in a bowl and leave for 10 minutes. Put the flour into a bowl and mix in the butter. Mix in the yeast and water, then knead well on a flat surface until smooth and elastic. Put the dough in a bowl, cover and leave in a warm place to double in size. Divide the dough into 14 portions, rolling each into a ball. Have ready 14 small squares of oiled greaseproof paper, and the filling. Using a small rolling pin, roll out each ball on a floured board into a circle 4 in (10 cm) in diameter. The centre of the circle should be about double the thickness of the edge. Put 1 tablespoon of the lotus seed paste in the centre of the round, then gently draw up the edges. Close the tops by pinching and twisting the dough. Place, sealed side down, on the pieces of oiled paper. Make a small incision in the top of each and leave to prove in a warm place until well risen – about 45 minutes. Arrange in a steamer so that they do not touch, and steam over a high heat for 15 minutes. Serve warm.

Black Bean Bao and Walnut Sesame Bao — Makes 14

China

Follow the recipe above but substitute one of the following two fillings for the lotus seed paste.

Black bean

1 lb (450 g) black bean paste
8 oz (225 g) sugar
2 oz (50 g) butter, softened

Walnut sesame

6 oz (175 g) ground walnuts
2 oz (50 g) sesame seeds
1 oz (25 g) butter, softened
8 oz (225 g) sugar
2 tablespoons (30 ml) oil

For each filling, fry the ingredients together for 15 minutes over a gentle heat. Allow to stand for 1 hour or until completely cool. They are now ready to use.

Vegetable Bao   *Makes 14*

China

1 tablespoon (15 ml) vegetable oil
1 tablespoon (15 ml) chopped spring onions
1 teaspoon finely chopped root ginger
3 oz (75 g) bamboo shoots, finely chopped
1 teaspoon crushed garlic
1 teaspoon sesame seeds
3 oz (75 g) carrot, grated
1 teaspoon (5 ml) chilli sauce
1 tablespoon (15 ml) sesame oil
1 quantity of bao dumpling dough (see Lotus Seed Bao recipe)

Heat the vegetable oil in a frying pan and stir fry the onions and ginger for 30 seconds. Add the next five ingredients and stir fry briskly for a further 30 seconds. Remove from the heat and mix in the sesame oil. Cool the mixture, then prepare and fill the bao and steam them as in the Lotus Seed Bao recipe.

Stocks and Soups

In Far Eastern cuisine soups are not normally served at the beginning of a meal but at the same time as the other dishes; the recipes given here may be used in either way. Far Eastern soups may be roughly divided into two categories. Firstly, there are thin soups, with only two or three carefully chosen ingredients floating in them; these lighter soups provide visual and gastronomic refreshment between main dishes. Secondly, there are thicker, more substantial soups such as those containing noodles, which can double as light meals in themselves or as one of the main courses at dinner.

Soup recipes show clearly the differences between the cooking styles of the different countries. Indonesian soups are hot or soured with tamarind or lemon juice. Thai soups are also hot, but flavoured with coriander seeds or leaves. Japanese soups are mildly flavoured but beautifully garnished, while Chinese soups contain elements of each of the other three.

Basic Vegetable Broth/Stock

Thai Stock

Japanese Stock

Noodle and Chinese Cabbage Soup

Mushroom and Coriander Soup

Chinese Greens and Coriander Soup

Chinese Egg Drop Soup

Lemon, Beancurd and Coconut Milk Soup

Spinach and Ginger Soup

Bamboo Shoot and Green Bean Soup

Vegetarian Shark's Fin Soup

Ginger and Mushroom Soup

Vegetable Soup with Rice Flour Dumplings

Thick Rice Soup

Four Fruits Soup

Miso and Vegetable Soup

Chilled Summer Vegetable Soup

Watercress Soup

Clear Soup with Lemon and Beancurd

Vegetable Stocks

The quality of the stock used in a soup makes all the difference between a good soup or a mediocre one. The stockpot is also a good way of using up trimmings, leftovers, the good bits of partially bad vegetables, and small amounts of dried beans or lentils. Three different Far Eastern stock recipes are given below. They are essentially all variations on the same theme.

Some of the vegetables you can use in soup stocks are: beansprouts, broccoli, cabbage, carrots, cauliflower, celery, Chinese greens, courgettes, green beans, leeks, onions, parsnips, pea pods, potatoes, spinach leaves, spring onions, turnips, watercress (including stems).

Basic Vegetable Broth/Stock   Makes 1½ pts (800ml)

China

2 pints (1 litre) water
1½ lb (700 g) vegetables
   consisting of 3 or all of the
   following:
   carrots
   celery
   leeks
   onions
   parsnips
   potatoes
   tomatoes
   turnips
8 oz (225 g) mushroom stalks
8 oz (225 g) dried butter beans
2 tablespoons (30 ml) soya sauce

Bring all the ingredients except the soya sauce to the boil in a large pan, and simmer together for 2–2½ hours. Then add the soya sauce and simmer for another 10 minutes. Strain and use for broth or stock.

Variations
As this stock takes some time to make, here are some simpler and faster versions:
1. Dissolve 1 vegetable stock cube and 1 teaspoon vegetable concentrate in 1¼ pints (700 ml) water.

2. Add 1 tablespoon (15 ml) soya sauce, 1 teaspoon Marmite (yeast extract) and 1½ teaspoons vegetable concentrate to 1¼ pints (700 ml) hot water. Stir until dissolved.

Thai Stock   Makes 2 pints (1.1 litres)

1½ lb (700 g) mixed root and
   green vegetables (see
   suggestions above)
3 pints (1.7 litres) water
8 oz (225 g) mushrooms with
   stems, sliced (*or* just stems
   may be used)
1 teaspoon salt
2 teaspoons (10 ml) light soya sauce
½ teaspoon sugar

Put the vegetables, water, mushrooms and salt in a large pan and bring to the boil. Reduce the heat, cover, and simmer for 45 minutes. Strain the stock through a fine sieve and return it to the pan. Boil it down to 2 pints (1.1 litres) and then stir in the soya sauce and sugar.

Japanese Stock

Makes 2½ pints (1.4 litres)

1½ lb (700 g) mixed root and green vegetables (see suggestions above)
6 oz (175 g) soya beans, soaked overnight and drained
3 pints (1.7 litres) water
1 teaspoon miso *or* yeast extract
salt, black pepper (*or* togarashi) and soya sauce to taste

Place the vegetables, beans and water in a large pan, add the miso and bring to the boil. Season to taste with salt, black pepper and soya sauce. Reduce the heat, cover, and simmer for 2–3 hours. Strain off the stock, adjust the seasoning and it's ready for use.

Noodle and Chinese Cabbage Soup

Serves 6

A vegetable version of a popular Thai soup, this recipe can be made with most types of noodles.

6 oz (175 g) dried egg noodles
1 tablespoon (15 ml) vegetable oil
3 cloves garlic, crushed
2 pints (1.1 litres) vegetable stock
8 oz (225 g) Chinese cabbage *or* other Chinese greens, thinly sliced
soya sauce to taste

4 oz (100 g) beansprouts
garnish
1 tablespoon chopped coriander leaves
2 oz (50 g) roasted peanuts, coarsely crushed
1–2 fresh *or* dried red chillies, seeded and finely chopped
½–1 tablespoon white sugar

Cook the noodles, in plenty of boiling water, according to the instructions on the packet or until just tender. Drain them and rinse under cold water until cooled to room temperature. Set them aside. Heat the oil in a large saucepan and sauté the garlic golden. Add the stock and bring to the boil. Put in the cabbage and simmer for 2 minutes. Add soya sauce to taste. Stir in the beansprouts and noodles and simmer until the noodles are heated through. Pour the soup into a tureen and sprinkle over the top the coriander leaves, peanuts, chilli peppers and sugar. Serve immediately.

Mushroom and Coriander Soup

Serves 4–6

This soup and the cabbage soup below are simple Thai peasant dishes. They are quick to make and tasty if you have a good stock available.

1 tablespoon (15 ml) vegetable oil
2 cloves garlic, crushed
½ teaspoon ground coriander seeds
¼ teaspoon freshly ground black pepper
2 teaspoons (10 ml) soya sauce
2 pints (1.1 litres) vegetable stock
4–6 medium mushrooms, wiped and thinly sliced

garnish
2 spring onions, finely chopped
1 tablespoon finely chopped coriander leaves
1 fresh *or* dried red chilli, seeded and thinly sliced (optional)

Heat the oil in a large saucepan and stir in the garlic, coriander and black pepper. Fry, stirring, until the garlic just turns golden. Add the soya sauce and stock and bring to a low simmer. Simmer for 10 minutes, then add the mushrooms. Simmer for a further 5 minutes, and then serve the soup garnished with chopped spring onion, coriander leaves and, if you like hot food, chilli pepper rings as well.

Variation
Replace the mushrooms with 4–6 Chinese dried mushrooms soaked in hot water for 30 minutes, drained, stems removed and discarded, and the caps sliced.

Chinese Greens and Coriander Soup   Serves 4–6

Follow the main recipe above, but replace the mushrooms with 10 oz (275 g) cabbage or Chinese cabbage, thinly sliced. After adding the cabbage, simmer for 6–7 minutes or until the cabbage is tender.

Variation
Towards the end of the cooking time add to the soup 12 oz (350 g) beancurd, cut into 1 in (2.5 cm) cubes, and heat through before serving.

Chinese Egg Drop Soup   Serves 4

1 egg
½ teaspoon (2.5 ml) water
1¼ pints (700 ml) vegetable stock
pinch sugar
pinch salt
few drops sesame oil
1 large shallot, chopped

garnish
2 teaspoons finely chopped chives

Beat the egg with the water in a small bowl. Bring the stock to a simmer and stir in the sugar, salt and sesame oil. Continue to stir and pour the egg into the simmering stock. As you stir the egg will coagulate and form thin threads. Stir in the shallot and remove from the heat. Pour the soup into individual bowls. Garnish with chives and serve.

Lemon, Beancurd and Coconut Milk Soup   *Serves 4*

A Thai-inspired creamy soup with a coconut and lemon flavour.

¾ pint (450 ml) water
¾ pint (450 ml) medium coconut milk
2 teaspoons grated lemon rind *or* finely chopped lemon grass
2 spring onions, finely chopped
½–1 fresh *or* dried red chilli, seeded and finely chopped
12 oz (350 g) beancurd cut into 1 in (2.5 cm) cubes
2 tablespoons (30 ml) lemon juice
2 tablespoons (30 ml) soya sauce

garnish
1 tablespoon finely chopped coriander leaves

Combine the water and coconut milk in a large saucepan and bring to a slow boil. Add the lemon rind and simmer for 10 minutes. Add the spring onions and chilli and simmer for a further 2–3 minutes. Stir in the beancurd, lemon juice and soya sauce. Heat the beancurd through, and serve the soup garnished with coriander leaves.

Spinach and Ginger Soup   *Serves 4*

This is a tasty and quick-to-prepare Indonesian soup. Chinese leaves or watercress may be substituted for the spinach.

2 tablespoons (30 ml) vegetable oil
1 in (2.5 cm) piece root ginger, finely chopped
1 oz (25 g) raw peanuts, dry roasted and crushed *or* 1½ teaspoons crunchy peanut butter
1½ pints (825 ml) boiling vegetable stock *or* water
10 oz (275 g) fresh spinach, finely chopped
1 teaspoon cornflour
½ teaspoon ground turmeric
1 tablespoon (15 ml) dark soya sauce
½ teaspoon dark brown sugar
salt and pepper to taste

Heat the oil in a saucepan, add the ginger and stir fry it gently for 2 minutes. Add the crushed peanuts and stir fry for 1 minute. Pour in the boiling stock, add the spinach and set the pan to simmer, covered, for 5 minutes. Combine in a small bowl the cornflour, turmeric, soya sauce, sugar, salt and pepper to taste and 2 tablespoons (30 ml) of stock from the soup. Make the mixture into a paste and stir this into the soup, leaving it to simmer, covered, for a further 10 minutes. Adjust the seasoning and serve.

Variation
To pep up the soup in the Indonesian manner add 1–2 finely chopped chilli peppers when you cook the ginger.

Bamboo Shoot and Green Bean Soup   Serves 6

This Indonesian soup is served with boiled rice. Some of the soup stock is used to moisten the rice, the soup vegetables are then spooned over it and the stock is served in a separate bowl. Vegetables other than green beans can be used: see variations below.

2 pints (1.1 litres) vegetable stock
1 medium onion, finely diced
2 cloves garlic, crushed
1 in (2.5 cm) piece root ginger, finely chopped
1 lb (450 g) tomatoes
2 bay leaves *or* daun salem leaves
1 lb (450 g) green beans, topped, tailed and cut into 2 in (5 cm) lengths
4 oz (100 g) tinned bamboo shoots, sliced
1 tablespoon (15 ml) lemon juice *or* tamarind water
salt and pepper to taste

Heat the stock in a pan and add the onion, garlic and ginger. Bring to the boil, cover and set to simmer. Scald the tomatoes briefly in boiling water, remove the skins and chop them into quarters. Put the tomatoes into the stock pan, add the bay leaves, stir well and season to taste with salt and pepper. Leave the soup to simmer for another 15 minutes. Add the green beans and bamboo shoots, stir well and return the pan to the boil. Reduce the heat to low and simmer, covered, for 15–20 minutes or until the beans are very tender. Stir in the lemon juice, adjust the seasoning and serve with boiled rice.

Variations

1. Substitute carrots, potatoes, courgettes, aubergines, cabbage etc. for the green beans.

2. Replace the bamboo shoots with sliced water chestnuts.

Vegetarian Shark's Fin Soup   Serves 4–6

China

4 Chinese dried mushrooms
¾ oz (20 g) silk noodles
½ oz (15 g) Chinese Szechwan preserved vegetables (optional)
2 oz (50 g) bamboo shoots
1 sheet dried beancurd
vegetable oil for deep frying

1 oz (25 g) green peas (if frozen, defrost completely)
1¾ pints (1 litre) good vegetable stock

thickening paste

1 tablespoon potato flour
2 tablespoons (30 ml) water

Soak the dried mushrooms in hot water for 30 minutes. Drain, discard the hard stalks, and cut the caps into thin slices. Dip the silk noodles into boiling water to soften, then cut into 5 in (12 cm) lengths. Soak for a further 10 minutes in cold water, then drain well. Rinse the preserved vegetables and cut them and the bamboo shoots into matchsticks. Deep fry the beancurd sheet over a moderate heat until crisp, then drain and crumble onto a plate. Heat 2 tablespoons (30 ml) vegetable oil in a large saucepan and stir fry the mushrooms, bamboo shoots, preserved vegetables and peas for 30 seconds. Add the stock and bring to the boil. Stir in the crumbled beancurd and drained silk noodles. Mix the potato flour paste with the water and stir this paste into the soup. Season to taste. Serve very hot in large bowls.

Ginger and Mushroom Soup   Serves 4

This distinctive Chinese soup, with its exotic ingredients and flavours, is excellent for dinner parties or other special occasions.

4 Chinese dried mushrooms
½ oz (12 g) snow fungus
2 squares dried beancurd
vegetable oil for deep frying
1 in (2.5 cm) piece root ginger, chopped
1 pint (550 ml) good vegetable stock
1 tablespoon (15 ml) peanut oil
1–2 teaspoons (5–10 ml) soya sauce
salt to taste
garnish
1 stick celery, finely chopped
1 teaspoon (5 ml) sesame oil

Wash the dried mushrooms well and soak in ⅓ pint (200 ml) hot water for 30 minutes. Discard the woody stalks and slice the caps thinly. Add the soaking water to the vegetable stock. Soak the snow fungus in separate hot water also for 30 minutes. Rinse well and cut into thin strips. Soften the beancurd with warm water and then pat dry in a teatowel. Deep fry in moderately hot oil for 30 seconds. Crumble the beancurd onto a plate. Heat the peanut oil in a pan. Stir fry the mushrooms, snow fungus and ginger for 30 seconds. Add the stock and bring to the boil. Season with the soya sauce and salt, stir in the crumbled beancurd and pour into a large serving bowl. Sprinkle the celery and sesame oil over the top and serve.

Vegetable Soup with Rice Flour Dumplings   *Serves 4*

Rice flour dumplings are easy to make and they add substance and interest to an otherwise ordinary Far Eastern soup.

2 tablespoons (30 ml) vegetable oil
8 oz (225 g) white radish (daikon) *or* baby turnips, peeled and diced
2–3 leaves Chinese cabbage *or* other leafy vegetable, coarsely shredded
1¾ pints (1 litre) stock
8 oz (225 g) rice flour
¼ pint (150 ml) boiling water
salt to taste
garnish
sprigs of parsley *or* mint *or* coriander

Heat the oil in a large saucepan and sauté the white radish until softened. Add the Chinese cabbage and stock and bring to the boil. Reduce the heat, cover, and simmer for 20 minutes. While the soup is cooking, prepare the rice dumplings. Carefully add to the rice flour, stirring vigorously with a wooden spoon, as much boiling water as necessary to produce quite a stiff dough. Knead the dough for 3–4 minutes and then remove small portions and roll into dumplings. Season the soup with salt and drop in the dumplings. At first they will sink to the bottom of the pan, but as they cook through (2–3 minutes) they will rise to the surface. To serve, garnish each bowl with sprigs of fresh herbs.

Thick Rice Soup   *Serves 4–6*

This is a warming soup from Japan.

2 pints (1.1 litres) stock
3 oz (75 g) long *or* short grain rice
2 teaspoons grated root ginger
salt and black pepper to taste

4 oz (100 g) green peas (frozen peas, defrosted, are suitable)
1 egg yolk, beaten
garnish
1 sheet nori seaweed (optional)

Bring the stock, rice and ginger to the boil. Reduce the heat, cover, and simmer until the rice is well cooked and starting to disintegrate (30 minutes for white rice, 1–1½ hours for brown rice). Season with salt and pepper and stir in the peas and egg yolk. Heat through, stirring, and then set to simmer for 5 minutes. Serve with toasted nori crumbled over the top. Toast the nori by holding the sheet over a low flame and moving it backwards and forwards for several seconds.

Four Fruits Soup   *Serves 4*

China
There is a wide range of preserved and dried fruits from China and Taiwan, including crystallized white melon, 'dehydrated' papaya and pineapple, preserved kumquats, apples, plums and red dates without stones; none of these needs soaking before use. There are also dried red and black dates, which need soaking for several hours before use.

2 oz (50 g) pearl barley
14 dried red dates
1 oz (25 g) glutinous rice

3 oz (75 g) mung beans, soaked overnight and drained
3 pints (1.7 litres) water
sugar to taste

Soak the barley, red dates and rice separately for 3 hours in cold water, then rinse well and drain. Remove the stones from the dates and chop the fruit into small pieces. Put all the ingredients into a pan with water. Boil gently for 1½ hours. Add sugar to taste, and serve hot or cold.

Miso and Vegetable Soup *Serves 4–6*

Miso soup is nutritious and good for the digestive system. It is a popular soup in Japan, where it is often served with rice for breakfast.

2 tablespoons (30 ml) vegetable oil
4 oz (100 g) white radish (daikon) *or* baby turnips, finely chopped into matchsticks
1 small onion, finely chopped
4 oz (100 g) carrots, thinly sliced
2 oz (50 g) mushrooms, sliced
3 oz (75 g) miso
2 pints (1.1 litres) stock *or* water
garnish
sprigs of parsley *or* 1 sheet nori seaweed

Heat the oil in a heavy pan and sauté the radish, onion and carrots until just softened. Stir in the mushrooms and sauté for a further 1–2 minutes. Cream the miso with a little of the stock and add the remaining stock to the pan. Bring to the boil and stir in the creamed miso. Return the soup to a low boil and simmer until the vegetables are cooked. Serve garnished with parsley sprigs or toasted nori. Toast the nori by holding the sheet over a low flame and moving it backwards and forwards for several seconds.

Chilled Summer Vegetable Miso Soup *Serves 4*

Japan

1¾ pints (1 litre) stock, chilled
3 oz (75 g) miso
4 oz (100 g) cucumber, thinly sliced and chilled
4 oz (100 g) tomatoes, diced and chilled
garnish
small bunch fresh mint, chopped

Blend the stock and miso together. Divide the vegetables among 4 bowls, pour the soup over them and garnish with mint.

Watercress Soup *Serves 4*

This is a simple but nutritious Chinese soup. For a more substantial version see the mushroom variation below.

1¾ pints (1 litre) stock
¼ teaspoon salt
1 tablespoon (15 ml) soya sauce
1 teaspoon sugar
1 teaspoon grated root ginger
1 large bunch watercress, leaves and fine stems only, cut into sprigs
2 spring onions, finely chopped

Combine the stock, salt, soya sauce, sugar and ginger in a saucepan and bring to the boil. Reduce the heat, cover, and simmer for 15 minutes. Return to a fast boil and add the watercress and spring onions. Simmer for a further 2–3 minutes and serve immediately.

Variation
Add 4–5 Chinese dried black mushrooms (soaked for 30 minutes in hot water, drained, stems removed and discarded, and the caps sliced) to the stock mixture before it is set to simmer, and increase the simmering time to 20 minutes.

Clear Soup with Lemon and Beancurd — *Serves 4*

Japan
A simple but tasty and visually attractive soup.

1¾ pints (1 litre) clear soup stock
6 oz (175 g) beancurd, cut into ½ in (1.25 cm) cubes
1 lemon, thinly sliced
1 small leek *or* 2 spring onions, finely chopped

Bring the stock to the boil and add the beancurd. Reduce the heat and simmer for a few minutes. Divide the soup and beancurd among 4 bowls, taking care not to crush the beancurd. Decorate each bowl with slices of lemon and leek. Do not crowd the bowls with ingredients. If you have too much lemon or leek, save it for future use.

Variation
For clear soup with ginger and beancurd, replace the lemon slices with 2 teaspoons finely chopped root ginger.

Pickles, Salads and Dressings

Pickles play an important role in Far Eastern cuisine, and the appetizing smell of pickled vegetables is a distinctive aroma in most Far Eastern markets. With their strong flavour and crisp texture, pickles add sparkle to peasant meals that may otherwise be bland and a little boring. They are also eaten as appetizers with small snacks and drinks. The two most common pickling agents are salt and vinegar, although miso is also used in Japan. In some of the pickling processes the maturation time is 2–3 months, but here I have mainly chosen quick pickling methods. Note: it is inadvisable to cook with vinegar in an aluminium pan.

Salads have a different meaning in the Far East from that understood in the West – a 'salad' may be anything from pickled vegetables to a dish of partially cooked vegetables with a dressing. I have chosen a cross-section of types, but I have concentrated more on recipes that fulfil our understanding of a salad – that is, fresh raw vegetables in a dressing. The salads given here may be used as starters, as side dishes or, in some cases, as main courses. A selection of them would make a notable contribution to a buffet meal.

The dressing recipes relate to particular salads in the text, but they may of course be tried with salads of your own choice.

Pickles

Thai Pickled Mixed Vegetables

Pickled Chilli Peppers

Cucumber Relish

Japanese Quick Pickles:
1. Mixed Vegetable (Salt Pressed) Pickle
2. Mixed Vegetable (Vinegar Pressed) Pickle
3. Sweet White Radish or Turnip Pickle
4. Pickled Melon

Vic's Viking Cucumber Pickle

Vic's Viking Mustard Mixed Pickle

Szechwan Pickled Vegetables

Preserved Red Ginger

Chinese Pickled Ginger

Mild Fresh Chinese Pickled Cucumber

Salads

Cooked Vegetable Salad in Coconut Sauce

Vegetable Salad with Hot Sauce

Grapefruit and Coconut Salad

Cucumber Salad (Indonesian)

Cucumber Salad (Thai)

Indonesian Fruit Salad

Carrot and Apple Salad

White Salad

Spinach Salad

Fried Aubergine Salad

Cucumber and Wakame Salad

Mixed-up Beansprout Salad

Beansprout and Cucumber Salad

Chinese Greens with Peanut Dressing

Spinach Salad with Sesame Seed and Soya Dressing

Orange and White Vinegared Salad

Apples and Grapes with Japanese Mustard Dressing

Dressings
Beancurd Dressing

Japanese Mustard Dressing

Japanese White Dressing

Sesame Seed and Soya Dressing

Pickles

Thai Pickled Mixed Vegetables   *Makes 3 pints (1.8 litres)*

Pickled vegetables in the Thai manner may be served as soon as they are made and still warm, or from the refrigerator where, stored in an airtight jar, they will keep for up to 2 weeks. A variety of vegetables are suitable for pickling. Select a combination from those suggested that suits availability and your own tastes.

1 pint (550 ml) cider vinegar *or* rice vinegar
1 tablespoon white sugar
1 teaspoon salt
1 lb (450 g) total weight of one or a combination of the following vegetables:
   broccoli, cut into bite-size pieces
   cabbage (white *or* spring), chopped into 1½ in (4 cm) squares
   carrots, peeled and cut into bite-size pieces
   cauliflower, cut into bite-size pieces
   celery, cut into bite-size pieces
   Chinese cabbage (including baak choi and Peking) chopped into 1½ in (4 cm) squares
   corn kernels, cut fresh from the cob
   cucumber, peeled, seeded and cut into bite-size pieces
   green beans, cut into bite-size pieces
6 cloves garlic, finely chopped
6 red chillies (use fewer for a less fiery pickle), seeded and finely chopped
6 shallots *or* 1 onion, finely diced
6 fl oz (175 ml) peanut oil *or* sesame oil
1 oz (25 g) sesame seeds, dry roasted light brown

Heat the vinegar, sugar and salt in a large saucepan and cook the chosen vegetables in the mixture individually. Remove them just before they are tender so that some 'bite' remains in the texture. Set them aside.

In a food blender or with a pestle and mortar grind the garlic, chillies and shallots into a paste. Add a little of the oil if the paste is too thick to remove from the blender goblet. Heat the remaining oil in a wok or frying pan and fry the paste, stirring, for 2–3 minutes. Add the vegetables and stir fry over a high heat for 30 seconds. Pour the contents of the pan into a serving dish and sprinkle with toasted sesame seeds. Serve immediately, or allow to cool and store in clean glass preserving jars in the refrigerator.

Pickled Chilli Peppers *Makes ½ pint (275 ml)*

Thailand
Pickled chillies are useful for adding a little fire to mildly flavoured dishes. They keep well and make a colourful alternative to dried chillies and/or chilli sauce for seasoning and garnishing.

6 fresh red chillies, seeded and thinly sliced
4 tablespoons (60 ml) rice vinegar *or* cider vinegar
4 fl oz (100 ml) water
¼ teaspoon salt
½ teaspoon white sugar

Combine all the ingredients in a clean glass jar. Store in the refrigerator and use as required. The chillies will keep for up to a month.

Cucumber Relish *Serves 4–6*

Indonesia
Delicious as an accompaniment to rice dishes and curries, and also excellent with cheese and salad.

1 medium cucumber, peeled, halved lengthwise, seeded and coarsely grated
1 tablespoon finely diced onion
1–2 fresh red chillies (fewer for a less fiery relish), seeded and finely chopped
1 teaspoon sugar
1 tablespoon (15 ml) lemon *or* lime juice
1 tablespoon (15 ml) soya sauce

Mix all the ingredients together in a bowl, and serve immediately

Japanese Quick Pickles
1. Mixed Vegetable (Salt Pressed) Pickle

4 cabbage leaves, finely chopped
2½ tablespoons salt
2 baby turnips, quartered and finely chopped
2 medium carrots, chopped into matchsticks
grated peel of 1 lemon

Put the cabbage leaves in a colander, sprinkle them with ½ tablespoon salt and stand to drain for 20–30 minutes. Press the leaves gently and squeeze out as much moisture as possible (this ensures that the pickled cabbage stays crisp). Combine the cabbage leaves, remaining salt, turnips, carrots and lemon peel in a salad bowl (glass, ceramic or wooden) and place a wooden lid or plate on top of the mixture. Weight the lid down with scale weights or a water-filled pan or jar weighing about 1½ lb (700 g). Leave for 2–24 hours in the refrigerator. The longer you leave the pickles weighted down, the more sour their taste. Pour off excess liquid as it collects. Rinse them in plenty of cold water and serve with soya sauce and grated ginger as accompaniments to main dishes. They will keep for up to 5 days in the refrigerator.

2. Mixed Vegetable (Vinegar Pressed) Pickle

1 lb (450 g) mixed vegetables (e.g. carrots, thinly sliced; cucumber, thinly sliced; red or green peppers, seeded and cut into strips; aubergines, cubed, salted and rinsed)
10 fl oz (300 ml) rice vinegar *or* cider vinegar
2 tablespoons sugar
2 teaspoons salt
1 tablespoon sesame paste

Prepare the vegetables. Combine the vinegar, sugar, salt and sesame paste and gently heat to dissolve the sugar. Combine the vegetables and the vinegar solution in a salad bowl (glass, ceramic or wood) and place a wooden lid or plate on top of the mixture. Weight the plate down with a scale weight or a water-filled jamjar and place in the refrigerator for 2–3 hours. The vegetable pickle is now ready to be served. Leave whatever is not used in the pickling liquid and transfer to a preserving jar with a non-metallic lid. Use as required. It will keep in the refrigerator for at least a couple of weeks.

3. Sweet White Radish or Turnip Pickle

2 lb (900 g) white radish *or* baby turnips
salt

4 fl oz (100 ml) rice vinegar *or* cider vinegar
8 oz (225 g) sugar

Wash the vegetables and slice crosswise into neat ⅛ in (0.3 cm) thick circles. Place in a colander and sprinkle with salt, ensuring that it is evenly distributed throughout. Leave for 1 hour, then rinse and squeeze dry in a clean cloth. Transfer to a storage jar with a non-metallic lid and pour the vinegar and sugar over them. Stir well. Refrigerate and use as required.

4. Pickled Melon

Once, when I visited a friend's house in Japan, his father invited me to taste his home-made wine. It turned out to be a jar full of garlic cloves covered with sake, sealed and left for a year or two. I had a small glass. The taste is hard to describe, but I can still remember it. Fortunately, pickled melon has a much different taste, even though it uses the same pickling agent.

1 small melon, peeled, seeded and cut into 1 in (2.5 cm) cubes
½ pint (275 ml) sake *or* medium sweet sherry

2 tablespoons (30 ml) brandy
pinch salt

Put the melon cubes into a sterilized preserving jar with a non-metallic lid. Add the other ingredients, seal and leave for at least 3 days. Serve as a dessert. You may need to add more sake and brandy if the amount given does not cover the melon.

Vik's Viking Cucumber Pickle *Serves 8–10*

The recipes for this pickle and the mixed pickle that follows are from the famous Vik's Viking restaurant in Jakarta, where they serve a huge and delicious array of dishes in a help-yourself buffet. The cucumber pickle is very soothing to the tongue after a dish hot with chillies.

2 lb (900 g) small pickling cucumbers
2 fresh large red chillies, seeded
2 fl oz (50 ml) white vinegar
4 fl oz (100 ml) water
1 lb (450 g) white sugar
1 teaspoon salt

Blanch the cucumbers and chillies in boiling water for a few seconds, then remove them and drain. Cut the cucumbers crosswise into ½ in (1 cm) thick slices. Cut the chillies once lengthwise, and then slice them thinly crosswise. Combine all the ingredients in a bowl and leave them, uncovered, for 3–5 hours. Stir occasionally. At first there will not be enough liquid to cover the cucumbers, but slowly liquid from the cucumbers will seep out and rise up the bowl. Store unused pickle in clean, airtight glass jars in the refrigerator.

Vik's Viking Mustard Mixed Pickle   Serves 8–10

8 oz (225 g) small pickling cucumbers, cut into ½ in (1 cm) thick slices
8 oz (225 g) shallots, peeled and cut into halves
8 oz (225 g) carrots, peeled and cut lengthwise into matchsticks
8 oz (225 g) cauliflower, cut into florets
2 fl oz (50 ml) white vinegar
4 fl oz (100 ml) water
1 lb (450 g) white sugar
1 tablespoon mustard powder
1 teaspoon salt

Blanch the cucumbers, shallots, carrots and cauliflower in boiling water for a few seconds, then remove them and drain. Combine all the ingredients in a bowl and leave uncovered for 3–5 hours. Stir occasionally. Store unused pickle in clean, airtight glass jars in the refrigerator.

Szechwan Pickled Vegetables

The following recipe for Chinese pickled vegetables is from Jack Santa Maria's very good book, *Chinese Vegetarian Cookery* (Rider). The author thanks him for permission to use it.

Here is the basic recipe. Choose vegetables in perfect condition. Wash and trim them, cutting them up where necessary. Put them in a large earthenware or stoneware pot which has a lid or bung. Add boiled water by the cup until the vegetables are covered by about 3 in (8 cm) of water. Sprinkle over them tablespoon salt for each cup of water used. Seal up the pot with wax or a flour and water paste, and leave to stand in a cool place for at least 2 weeks. You can add to the salt other spices, such as chilli powder, according to taste.

This pickle is very salty and spicy, but it can be soaked in water before use if a milder taste is preferred. It may be sliced and used as a pickle, stir fried with vegetables or beancurd, or used as an ingredient in soups.

Preserved Red Ginger   *Makes 1 pint (550 ml)*

China
Use for food decoration and flavour.

8 oz (225 g) fresh root ginger, thinly sliced and cut into thin strips 2 in (5 cm) long
1 tablespoon salt
¾ pint (450 ml) cider vinegar *or* wine vinegar

5 oz (150 g) granulated sugar
½ teaspoon (2.5 ml) red colouring

Sprinkle the ginger slices with the salt and leave them to stand for 2 hours. Rinse them thoroughly and drain. Heat the vinegar in a heavy saucepan and stir in the sugar until dissolved. Add the root ginger, cover, and simmer gently for about 10 minutes. Remove from the heat, add the food colouring and stir. Leave to cool completely. Put in a clean glass jar, cover and refrigerate. This preserved ginger will keep for about a year.

Chinese Pickled Ginger

Thin slices of pickled ginger are commonly used in Chinese stir fried dishes. Served with preserved duck eggs it is also a popular snack.

1 lb (450 g) root ginger, peeled
salt
¾ pint (450 ml) white vinegar

1 lb (450 g) white sugar
1 clove garlic, crushed

Put the ginger in a colander and liberally sprinkle it with salt. Leave it for 30 minutes, stirring it around 3 or 4 times during this period. Remove it from the colander and dab dry on paper towels. Combine the vinegar, sugar and garlic and bring to the boil gently. Simmer for 5 minutes and pour the solution over the ginger in a bowl. Set aside to cool. Transfer the ginger and pickling liquid to 2 pint (1.1 litre) preserving jars with non-metallic lids and put in the refrigerator until well chilled. Store the pickle in a cool place. It will be ready in 4–5 days, and will keep for up to a year.

Mild Fresh Chinese Pickled Cucumber   *Makes 1 lb (450 g)*

1 lb (450 g) firm cucumbers, sliced (and peeled if the skin is tough)
4 fl oz (100 ml) cider vinegar
1 teaspoon salt
1 teaspoon (5 ml) soya sauce

Bring the cider vinegar to the boil and pour it over the cucumbers in a bowl. Stir in the salt and soya sauce and allow the cucumbers to marinate in the refrigerator, tightly covered, for 2–3 days.

Variation
Onions, green beans or other crisp vegetables can be used in conjunction with the cucumbers.

Salads

Cooked Vegetable Salad in Coconut Sauce   *Serves 6*

Thai vegetable salad is a cooked, spicy vegetable dish served hot with rice and other dishes. The vegetables are cooked in coconut milk until just tender, and then mixed with a hot, lemon-flavoured paste. Any convenient combination from the selection of vegetables suggested may be used.

select 1½ lb (700 g) total weight of a combination of 3 or more of the following:
aubergines, cut into 2 in (5 cm) cubes
broccoli, cut into bite-size pieces
carrots, peeled and cut into rounds
cauliflower, cut into bite-size florets

¾ pint (450 ml) medium coconut milk
salt to taste
2 oz (50 g) creamed coconut
2 fl oz (50 ml) water
2 tablespoons finely chopped onion
2 cloves garlic
½ teaspoon ground coriander
1–3 chillies, seeded

Chinese cabbage (including baak choi, choi sum or Peking) cut into 2 in (5 cm) strips	2 teaspoons grated lemon peel *or* chopped lemon grass
French beans, cut into 2 in (5 cm) lengths	2 tablespoons (30 ml) lemon juice *or* tamarind water
green peppers, seeded and cut into 1 in (2.5 cm) strips	1 tablespoon coarsely ground roasted peanuts
turnips, cut into bite-size pieces	*garnish* 2 tablespoons chopped coriander leaves

Put the selected vegetables, coconut milk and ½ teaspoon salt in a saucepan and bring to a low boil. Reduce the heat and simmer until the vegetables are just tender. During this time dissolve the creamed coconut in the water in a small pan and bring to a slow simmer. Put the onion, garlic, coriander, chillies and lemon peel into a food blender and grind to a smooth paste. If necessary, add a little of the coconut milk from the vegetable pan to ensure smoothness. Transfer the paste to the simmering coconut cream and stir it in. Simmer, stirring, until the mixture starts to thicken as the water evaporates and oil from the coconut cream is released. Stir this paste, the lemon juice and ground peanuts into the vegetables in the pan. Transfer to a serving dish, garnish with coriander leaves and serve.

Vegetable Salad with Hot Sauce   *Serves 4 or more*

For this South East Asian salad suitably cut fresh vegetables are dipped into a hot sauce and then eaten in the manner of a French *crudité*. Select a number of vegetables from those suggested in the recipe, remembering to vary texture, colour and flavour. Present them arranged on a large serving dish around a bowl of the hot sauce.

aubergine slices, browned in a little oil
carrots, cut into sticks
celery, cut into sticks
chicory leaves
Chinese cabbage, coarsely chopped into strips
courgette slices, browned in a little oil
cucumber, sliced
green apples, sliced and sprinkled with lemon juice
green peppers, seeded and cut into strips
red radishes, whole
watercress, in sprigs
young green beans, left whole

sauce

2 tablespoons (30 ml) soya sauce
1 tablespoon finely chopped onion
3 cloves garlic
juice of 2 lemons
1 tablespoon sugar
chilli sauce to taste

Prepare all the vegetables and chill. Prepare the sauce by putting all the remaining ingredients into a blender and blending to a smooth sauce.

Grapefruit and Coconut Salad   Serves 4

Serve this Thai salad as a starter or side dish. If available, pomeloes may be substituted for grapefruit.

4 oz (100 g) desiccated coconut
1 teaspoon sugar
2 teaspoons (10 ml) soya sauce
2 tablespoons (30 ml) lemon juice *or* tamarind water
2 tablespoons (30 ml) water
2 teaspoons (10 ml) vegetable oil
1 clove garlic, crushed
2 tablespoons finely diced onion
2 large grapefruit, peeled and segmented

garnish
lettuce leaves

Dry roast the coconut in a frying pan until it just starts to brown. Turn it into a mixing bowl and stir in the sugar, soya sauce, lemon juice and water. Heat the oil in a small pan and stir fry the garlic and onion golden. Stir this mixture into the coconut. Arrange the grapefruit segments on a few lettuce leaves on individual plates. Pour some of the coconut dressing over each, and serve.

Cucumber Salad   *Serves 4*

Indonesia
Choose between two different dressings which you can use: the first is lemon-based and garlic-flavoured, while the second is vinegar-based and spiced with chilli powder.

½ medium cucumber, peeled
   and thinly sliced

lemon dressing
juice of 1 lemon
2 tablespoons (30 ml) vegetable oil
1 teaspoon sugar
2 cloves garlic, crushed
salt to taste

chilli dressing
2 tablespoons (30 ml) white vinegar
1 teaspoon sugar
¼ teaspoon chilli powder
1–2 spring onions, finely chopped

Combine the ingredients of either dressing and toss the cucumber slices in the mixture. Chill and serve.

Variation
Pluck the green sprigs of a bunch of watercress from the stalks, wash and drain them and combine with the cucumber salad.

Cucumber Salad   *Serves 4*

Thailand

1 medium cucumber, peeled, halved lengthwise, seeded and finely sliced
2 tablespoons finely diced onion
1 tablespoon finely chopped spring onion
juice of 1 lemon

1 tablespoon (15 ml) soya sauce
1 teaspoon sugar
¼ teaspoon (1.25 ml) chilli sauce
¼ teaspoon freshly ground black pepper

Combine the cucumber, onion and spring onion in a serving bowl. Mix the lemon juice, soya sauce, sugar, chilli sauce and black pepper together. Pour this dressing over the cucumber salad. Toss well and serve.

Indonesian Fruit Salad   *Serves 4*

In this unusual fruit salad, fruits and vegetables are combined and served with a dressing made with chillies, vinegar and plenty of brown sugar. Use any combination of fresh fruit or vegetables in season. A selection is given below. Serve the fruit salad on its own, as part of a larger meal alongside savoury dishes, or as the last course of a lunch.

2 Granny Smith apples, peeled and cut into pieces
2 oranges, peeled and segmented
1 grapefruit, peeled and segmented
½ fresh pineapple, peeled and cubed *or* 1 small tin pineapple
1–2 firm mangoes, peeled and cut into pieces
½ cucumber, sliced
1 bunch radishes, washed, topped and tailed

dressing
1 fresh or dried red chilli, seeded and finely chopped
1 tablespoon (15 ml) dark soya sauce
4 oz (100 g) dark brown sugar
2 tablespoons (30 ml) white vinegar *or* 2 tablespoons (30 ml) lemon juice

Combine all the fruits and vegetables in a large bowl. Mix the dressing ingredients by hand or in a blender, and then pour the dressing over the fruit salad. Toss well and serve. The dressing can also be served in individual bowls into which each fruit is dipped before eating.

Carrot and Apple Salad   *Serves 4*

Indonesia

8 oz (225 g) carrots, peeled and grated
8 oz (225 g) eating apples, grated

dressing
juice of 1 lemon
2 tablespoons (30 ml) vegetable oil (sesame seed *or* peanut oil are best)
salt and black pepper to taste

Mix the carrot and apple. In a separate bowl combine the lemon juice and oil and season it with salt and black pepper to make the dressing. Toss the carrot and apple mixture in the dressing and serve at once.

White Salad   Serves 4

White salad is a popular Japanese beancurd dish.

4 Chinese dried black mushrooms *or* Japanese shiitake (*or* 4 oz (100 g) fresh mushrooms, sliced)
2 medium carrots, peeled and chopped into matchsticks
4 fl oz (100 ml) stock *or* water
½ teaspoon salt
1 teaspoon (5 ml) soya sauce
beancurd dressing (*see* Dressings)
garnish
2 tablespoons chopped mint *or* coriander leaves

If you are using dried mushrooms, soak them in warm water for 30 minutes, remove and discard the stems, and slice the caps. In a small pan combine the mushrooms, carrots, stock, salt and soya sauce. Bring it to the boil and simmer, uncovered, until all the liquid has evaporated or been absorbed. Transfer the contents of the pan to a serving bowl and set aside to cool to room temperature. Stir in the beancurd dressing, garnish with chopped herbs and serve.

Spinach Salad   Serves 4

This Japanese salad is also good made with other greens such as lettuce, Chinese cabbage and broccoli.

1 lb (450 g) spinach, washed and drained
3 tablespoons sesame seeds, toasted and crushed (*or* 1½ tablespoons sesame paste *or* tahini)
2 tablespoons (30 ml) soya sauce
1 teaspoon (5 ml) white vinegar
1 teaspoon (5 ml) dry English mustard *or* wasabi
2 spring onions, finely chopped
2 teaspoons finely grated root ginger
½ teaspoon black pepper *or* togarashi

Pick over the spinach and cut away any coarse stems. Cook the spinach for about 3 minutes in boiling water. Drain, and gently press to remove excess water. Chop the spinach into approximately 2 in (5 cm) lengths. Combine the remaining ingredients and mix to a smooth paste. Serve the spinach and dressing warm in separate bowls.

Variation
Add to the cooked spinach 8 oz (225 g) stir fried bamboo shoots, cut into matchsticks.

Fried Aubergine Salad *Serves 4*

Japan

1 lb (450 g) aubergines, thinly sliced
salt
2 tablespoons (30 ml) vegetable oil

4 tablespoons (60 ml) Japanese Mustard Dressing (*see* Dressings)

Generously salt the aubergines, layer in a colander and leave to drain. Rinse, press out excess moisture and pat dry with a clean cloth. Heat the oil in a frying pan and fry the aubergine slices until nicely brown on both sides. Serve hot with Mustard Dressing.

Cucumber and Wakame Salad *Serves 4*

Wakame is now available in some health/wholefood shops and Japanese stores. It makes a nutritious and unusual salad ingredient.

4 oz (100 g) wakame seaweed
1 medium cucumber, thinly sliced
4 tablespoons (60 ml) white vinegar

2 tablespoons (30 ml) soya sauce
2 teaspoons sugar
½ teaspoon salt

Rinse the wakame and soak it in cold water for 20–30 minutes. Drain, gently squeeze out the excess moisture and cut it into 1½ in (3.75 cm) lengths. Mix it with the cucumber. Combine the last 4 ingredients and pour the mixture over the vegetables. Serve.

Mixed-up Beansprout Salad   Serves 4

This salad is called mixed up because it has Chinese, Indian and Indonesian origins, reflecting the culinary influences that have affected South East Asian cookery. Surprisingly, the mixed flavours work well and the salad is handy to make if you are short of fresh ingredients.

8 oz (225 g) beansprouts, washed and drained
4 oz (100 g) tinned water chestnuts, drained and sliced
4 oz (100 g) fresh (or tinned and drained) pineapple cubes
¼ teaspoon ground cumin
¼ teaspoon ground coriander
1 teaspoon (5 ml) soya sauce
3 tablespoons (45 ml) Beancurd Dressing (see Dressings)
garnish
pinch ground coriander

Combine the beansprouts, water chestnuts and pineapple and mix well. Stir the cumin, coriander and soya sauce into the dressing and pour the mixture over the salad. Toss well, garnish with a pinch of ground coriander and serve at once.

Beansprout and Cucumber Salad   Serves 4

This is a very simple but effective Indonesian salad. It contains no fat but the dressing is quite sweet. Replace the sugar with clear honey if you prefer its flavour. For a more robust dish, toss the finished salad with a handful of roasted unsalted peanuts.

8 oz (225 g) beansprouts, washed and drained
1 large cucumber, sliced in half lengthwise, seeded and cut into matchsticks
2 tablespoons finely diced spring onions
3 fl oz (75 ml) cider vinegar
1 tablespoon white sugar
½ teaspoon salt

Combine the beansprouts, cucumber and onion. Stir the vinegar, sugar and salt together until the sugar dissolves. Toss the salad in this dressing and serve.

Chinese Greens with Peanut Dressing   Serves 4

This salad is very good with Chinese flowering cabbage (choi sum), a green, leafy vegetable with a mild flavour which is very popular with the Chinese. It is available at most Chinese grocery stores all year round. If choi sum is unavailable, the same dressing is good with Chinese white cabbage (baak choi).

8 oz (225 g) Chinese cabbage, washed, trimmed if necessary, and tied into bundles
salt
2 tablespoons creamy peanut butter
1 tablespoon (15 ml) soya sauce

Drop the bundle of greens into a pan of lightly salted, slowly boiling water for 2 minutes. Drain the greens, pull the bundles apart and immediately rinse them under cold water until cooled.

Chop the greens into 1 in (2.5 cm) lengths. Mix together the peanut butter and soya sauce (add a little oil if the mixture is too thick). Toss the greens in this dressing and serve them in individual deep serving bowls.

Spinach Salad with Sesame Seed and Soya Dressing *Serves 4*

Japan

1 lb (450 g) spinach
salt
4 tablespoons (60 ml) Sesame Seed and Soya Dressing (*see* Dressings)

Wash the spinach leaves well. Bring a large pan of lightly salted water to the boil. Add the spinach and cook very briefly. As soon as the spinach droops, quickly drain it and rinse under cold water until cooled. Drain it well again and gently squeeze out excess water. Chop the spinach into about 1½ in (4 cm) lengths. Toss the spinach in the dressing and serve in deep individual serving bowls with the spinach resting in the centre of the bowl.

Orange and White Vinegared Salad *Serves 6*

Japan

This is a versatile salad that can be served as an appetizer, as a side dish with the main course, or on its own with drinks and salted nuts. The salad can be served within an hour of being prepared, but it is not at its best until at least 8 hours later. It keeps well for up to 2 weeks in an airtight container in the refrigerator, so it's worth making more than you immediately need.

8 oz (225 g) white radish (daikon)
2 medium carrots
1 teaspoon salt
3 fl oz (75 ml) rice vinegar *or* cider vinegar
1 teaspoon (5 ml) soya sauce
1 tablespoon white sugar

Peel the white radish and scrape the carrots; cut them both into matchsticks about 1½ in (4 cm) in length. Put them into a large mixing bowl and sprinkle with the salt. Leave for 30 minutes and then gather the radish/carrot mixture in both hands and gently squeeze out all the water you can.

Combine the vinegar, soya sauce and sugar and add the mixture to the vegetables. Cover and refrigerate. Serve, if you wish, after 1 hour, but the salad is at its best if left to mature, as mentioned above.

Apples and Grapes with Japanese Mustard Dressing
Serves 4

The large black muscat grapes available in Britain in early winter and around Christmas are excellent with this salad, which makes an unusual, appetizing, bitter-sweet starter.

8 oz (225 g) eating apples, cored and cut into small chunks
juice of ½ lemon
8 oz (225 g) large grapes, washed
2 tablespoons (30 ml) Japanese Mustard Dressing (*see* Dressings)
1 teaspoon mustard seeds

Sprinkle the apple with lemon juice and set aside to chill. Cut the grapes in half and pick out the seeds with the tip of a pointed knife. Lightly chill the grapes. Toss the apple pieces and grapes in the dressing and garnish with mustard seeds. Serve in individual bowls.

Dressings

Beancurd Dressing
Makes about 8 fl oz (225 ml)

6 oz (175 g) fresh beancurd, drained
1 tablespoon chopped onion
1 tablespoon (15 ml) olive oil *or* other vegetable oil
1 tablespoon (15 ml) water
1 tablespoon (5 ml) lemon juice
1 teaspoon (5 ml) honey
salt to taste

Place all the ingredients in a liquidizer or food processor. Blend together at high speed. Adjust the seasoning.

Japanese Mustard Dressing
Makes 4–5 tablespoons (60–75 ml)

1 teaspoon prepared English mustard *or* wasabi
2 tablespoons (30 ml) rice vinegar *or* cider vinegar
1 tablespoon (30 ml) soya sauce
1–2 teaspoons sugar

Combine the mustard, vinegar and soya sauce in a small mixing bowl, add sugar to taste and stir well to dissolve the sugar.

Japanese White Dressing
Makes ¼ pint (150 ml)

This has the consistency of mayonnaise and is used in Japanese cuisine as a dressing for raw and cooked salads. Make the dressing only as needed – it doesn't keep well.

5 oz (150 g) cake beancurd
2 tablespoons sesame seeds (*or* 1 tablespoon sesame paste *or* tahini)
1 tablespoon white sugar
½ teaspoon salt

Remove excess water from the beancurd to get a dressing of the right consistency. Wrap the beancurd in 2–3 layers of absorbent kitchen paper and place a small bowl full of water on top of it. Leave it for 30 minutes and then mash the pressed beancurd in a bowl. If using sesame seeds, dry roast them over a moderate heat until they are brown. Crush the seeds into a paste with a pestle and mortar and stir this or sesame paste into the beancurd. Add the sugar and salt and stir into a smooth consistency.

Variation
For Vinegared White Dressing, stir in 2 teaspoons (10 ml) rice vinegar or cider vinegar.

Sesame Seed and Soya Dressing   *Makes 4 fl oz (100 ml)*

This is a sweet-and-sour flavoured dressing which goes well with crunchy, flavoursome vegetables. Tahini or Chinese sesame paste may be used in place of the sesame seeds.

4 tablespoons sesame seeds (*or* 2 tablespoons sesame paste *or* tahini)
1 teaspoon sugar
2 teaspoons (10 ml) soya sauce

2 tablespoons (30 ml) water *or* stock
1 tablespoon (15 ml) rice vinegar *or* cider vinegar

Dry roast the sesame seeds over a moderate heat until they are golden brown. Crush the seeds into a paste with a pestle and mortar. Combine this or sesame paste with the remaining ingredients, and mix well to dissolve the sugar.

Vegetable Dishes

In Far Eastern cookery vegetables are always prepared with care, and whether they are cooked by stir frying, steaming, braising or another method, the cook is careful to ensure that the cooked vegetables retain their individual flavours, textures and colours. Vegetable dishes are seen not only as an accompaniment to a main course but as independent dishes judged for taste and visual appeal in their own right.

Vegetables should be cut to suit the manner in which they are to be cooked, and also in uniform sizes to ensure uniform cooking. In addition, the appearance of the cooked vegetables should be pleasing to the eye. Thus in mixed vegetable dishes cut some vegetables in rounds, others in matchsticks, others in cubes or rectangles and so on. One other factor to be borne in mind is that if the meal is to be eaten with chopsticks, each piece of food should be small enough to pick up and put in the mouth whole.

Recipes containing vegetables are to be found in nearly every chapter in the book, but this chapter contains recipes solely for vegetable-only dishes. There are several side dish recipes and the remainder are for main dishes. In many cases the vegetable or vegetable combination given in a particular recipe is only a suggestion and the cooking method given may be applied equally successfully to other vegetables or combinations. Like many recipes in this book, therefore, specific vegetable recipes may be followed exactly or used as a starting point for the expression of your own ideas and preferences.

Spicy Aubergines

Aubergines and Tomatoes Cooked with Soya Sauce

Fried Aubergines

Braised Aubergines with Peppers and Onions

Cos Lettuce in Cream Sauce

Green Beans with Sesame and Sherry Sauce

Spiced Stir Fried Green Beans

Stir Fried Watercress

Cucumber and Mushrooms

Chrysanthemum Turnips

Oden

Japanese Skewered Vegetables

Mixed Vegetable Salad with Coconut Sauce

Green Salad with Coconut Sauce

Hunan Vegetable Hotpot

Broccoli with Coconut and Lemon Sauce

Thai Curried Beancurd with Vegetables

Stir Fried Vegetables

Yellow and Green Summer Vegetables

Honey Glazed Mushrooms

Spicy Aubergines   Serves 4

Japan

1 lb (450 g) auberines cut into
  ¾ in (2 cm) cubes, salted,
  pressed, rinsed and drained
4 tablespoons (60 ml) vegetable
  oil
2 teaspoons finely grated root
  ginger
1 clove garlic, crushed
1 medium onion, finely sliced
pinch cayenne pepper *or*
  Japanese seven spices pepper

3 fl oz (75 ml) vegetable stock
  or water
1 teaspoon sugar
garnish
1 tablespoon finely chopped
  chives *or* parsley (*or* 1 sheet
  nori seaweed, toasted and
  crumbled)

Heat the oil in a heavy pan, add the aubergines and sauté for 3–4 minutes. Stir frequently. Remove the aubergines from the pan, drain and reserve the oil. Put the aubergines to one side and return the oil to the pan. Add the ginger, garlic, onion and cayenne and sauté over a high flame for 30 seconds. Reduce the heat, pour in the stock and sugar and mix well. Add the aubergines and bring to the boil. Turn off the heat and serve garnished with chives, parsley or nori.

Aubergines and Tomatoes
Cooked with Soya Sauce   Serves 4

Indonesia
Serve with boiled rice or as an accompaniment to other dishes.

2 medium aubergines, thickly
  sliced, each slice cut in half to
  form 2 semi-circles
salt
2 tablespoons (30 ml) vegetable
  oil
1 medium onion, sliced
2 cloves garlic, crushed

8 oz (225 g) ripe tomatoes,
  peeled and chopped *or* tinned
  tomatoes, chopped
½ teaspoon chilli powder
2 tablespoons (30 ml) dark soya
  sauce
2 teaspoons dark brown sugar
salt and pepper to taste

Sprinkle the aubergines liberally with salt and leave them in a colander to stand for 30 minutes. Rinse them under cold water and dry them on absorbent kitchen paper. Heat the oil in a saucepan over a moderate heat and sauté the onion and garlic until the onion is softened. Add the aubergines and sauté for 2–3 minutes. Add the remaining ingredients and mix well. Cover the pan and simmer for 10 minutes, stirring occasionally. Adjust the seasoning and serve.

Fried Aubergines *Serves 3–4*

Indonesia
Serve as a side dish or with salad and rice as a light meal.

2 medium aubergines
salt
3–4 tablespoons (45–60 ml) vegetable oil for frying

1 medium onion, finely sliced
paprika to taste

Slice the aubergines quite thickly, sprinkle the slices with salt and leave them in a colander to stand for 30 minutes. Rinse them under cold water and dry on absorbent kitchen paper. Heat the oil in a heavy frying pan or wok, and shallow fry the slices a few at a time until lightly browned and cooked. Drain the fried slices on absorbent paper. Meanwhile, fry the onion slices until crisp and brown. Combine the aubergines and fried onion and season with salt and paprika.

Braised Aubergines with Peppers and Onions *Serves 4 as a side dish or 2 as a main dish*

China
Serve as a side dish, or with rice as a main course.

2 tablespoons (30 ml) oil
1 medium aubergine, cut into large chunks
¼ pint (150 ml) water
2 cloves garlic, minced
1 tablespoon (15 ml) soya sauce

1 medium green pepper, seeded and cut into 1 in (2.5 cm) squares
1 small chilli, seeded and chopped
10 spring onions *or* 1 large onion, sliced

Heat the oil in a frying pan with a lid and brown the aubergine pieces on all sides over a moderate heat. Add the water, garlic, soya sauce and chilli and cover the pan. Reduce the heat and cook slowly for 10 minutes. When the aubergine is tender, add the green pepper and sliced onion. Cook for 2 more minutes, covered, with the heat increased to moderate. Check for tenderness; the aubergine should be fork-tender but not falling apart. Serve at once.

Green Beans

Young French or green beans topped and tailed, parboiled in a little salted water for 4–5 minutes, drained, immersed for a few minutes in cold water to preserve their colour, and served on their own make an excellent side dish. Green beans are also used in many Japanese recipes as a garnish, or as an ingredient in pickles or cold cooked salads.

Green Beans with Sesame and Sherry Sauce

Serves 4 as a side dish

Japan

12 oz (350 g) green beans cut diagonally into ½ in (1.25 cm) pieces
salt
1 tablespoon (15 ml) medium sweet sherry *or* mirin
4 tablespoons sesame seeds, dry roasted and crushed (*or* 2 tablespoons (30 ml) sesame paste *or* tahini)

1 tablespoon sugar
1 tablespoon (15 ml) soya sauce
2 tablespoons (30 ml) stock *or* water

Parboil the beans in boiling, salted water for 5 minutes. Drain, and distribute the beans among 4 individual serving dishes. Combine the sherry, sesame, sugar, soya sauce and stock and mix well together. Pour the sauce over the beans and serve.

Spiced Stir Fried Green Beans   *Serves 4 as a side dish*

Indonesia

2 tablespoons (30 ml) vegetable oil
12 oz (350 g) French *or* green beans, topped, tailed and cut into 2 in (5 cm) pieces
1 small onion, finely diced

2 cloves garlic, crushed
½ teaspoon (2.5 ml) hot pepper sauce
1 tablespoon (15 ml) dark soya sauce

Heat the oil in a wok or frying pan and stir fry the beans, onion and garlic for 2–3 minutes. Add the hot pepper sauce and soya sauce and stir fry a further minute. Remove the pan from the heat and serve.

Stir Fried Watercress   *Serves 3–4*

Watercress is one of the most abundant salad greens. It is very good served Chinese-fashion with bamboo shoots and mushrooms.

2 bunches fresh green watercress
6 Chinese dried black mushrooms
2 tablespoons (30 ml) vegetable oil
2 oz (50 g) bamboo shoots, shredded

salt to taste
1 teaspoon sugar
1 in (2.5 cm) piece root ginger, peeled and chopped
1 tablespoon (15 ml) brandy (optional)

Trim off and discard the tougher stems of watercress. Rinse and shake well. Put the mushrooms in a mixing bowl, add boiling water to cover and allow to stand for 30 minutes. Drain them, then squeeze to remove excess moisture. Cut off and discard the tough stalks, and finely chop the caps. Heat the oil in a frying pan or wok and add the bamboo shoots and mushrooms. Cook, stirring, over a high heat for about 1 minute. Add the watercress and stir. Add the salt, sugar and ginger and cook for 1 minute, stirring all the while. Add the brandy, if used, and cook for a further 5 seconds. Spoon the vegetables onto a serving dish, leaving any liquid in the pan. Reduce it over a high heat, then pour in the liquid that will have accumulated in the serving dish (rather a lot!). Reduce briefly, and pour over the vegetables.

Cucumber and Mushrooms *Serves 4 as a side dish*

Japan

1 medium cucumber, thinly sliced
salt
2 tablespoons (30 ml) vegetable oil
4 oz (100 g) mushrooms, sliced
3 tablespoons (45 ml) soya sauce
1 tablespoon sugar
garnish
2 tablespoons sesame seeds, dry roasted

Layer the cucumber slices in a colander and salt each layer. Allow to stand for 30 minutes, rinse, drain and dry on a clean cloth. Heat the oil in a heavy pan, then add the mushrooms and cucumber slices. Cook over a high heat, stirring occasionally, until both vegetables are tender (2–3 minutes). Remove from the heat. Stir in the soya sauce and sugar, and serve sprinkled with sesame seeds.

Chrysanthemum Turnips *Serves 2–4*

In this Japanese recipe the plain turnip is turned into a colourful flower! Serve the turnips as a side dish or as part of a salad.

2 baby turnips
3 tablespoons (45 ml) vinegar
1 tablespoon (15 ml) sugar
pinch salt
1 red pepper, minced *or* peel of 1 lemon, grated
chrysanthemum leaves *or* lettuce

Cut the stems off the turnips and peel the vegetables very finely. Stand them on their stem end and place a chopstick on each side of a turnip. Now cut as though you were cutting a whole turnip into thin slices, but stop each stroke as your knife meets a chopstick. Repeat across the other way to give a pine needle effect. Soak the turnips in salted water until softened (30 minutes–1 hour). Rinse, wipe dry on a clean cloth and stand in individual bowls. Combine the vinegar, sugar and salt and pour it over the turnips. Allow to stand for 2–3 hours. Decorate by topping with small circles cut out of the red pepper for red-centred chrysanthemums, or lemon peel for yellow-centred ones. Stand in a bed of chrysanthemum or lettuce leaves to give a flower effect.

Oden
Serves 6–8

A popular Japanese winter casserole, oden is often prepared for festive occasions when people help themselves out of the oden pot, which can bubble away all evening without spoiling. In some big cities vendors sell oden in the streets. From experience I can tell you they are not keen on customers who want to pick and choose from the oden pot. They believe in pot luck.

2 pints (1.1 litres) stock
1 tablespoon sugar
1 tablespoon (15 ml) soya sauce
2 medium carrots, cut into 2 in (5 cm) pieces
8 oz (225 g) baby turnips *or* daikon, chopped
8 oz (225 g) new potatoes, scrubbed
12 oz (350 g) pressed beancurd, cut into 2 in (5 cm) pieces
4 oz (100 g) cabbage, coarsely chopped
6 hardboiled eggs, shelled
salt to taste

Bring the stock to the boil in a large pot and add the sugar and soya sauce. Add the carrots, turnips and potatoes and simmer, covered, for 15 minutes. Add the beancurd, cabbage, boiled eggs and salt. Simmer, covered, for another 15 minutes or until all the vegetables are tender. Transfer the oden to a warmed tureen and serve.

Japanese Skewered Vegetables
Makes 4 kebabs

These vegetable kebabs can be cooked under a grill or over hot charcoal. Serve with rice or bread. Vegetables other than those suggested may be used, but make sure they all cook at approximately the same rate (adjust cooking times by parboiling, or by cutting the vegetables smaller or larger).

1 onion, quartered and each quarter halved
2 carrots, each cut into 4 pieces and parboiled in boiling salted water for 5 minutes
2 green peppers, cored, seeded and cut into approximately 2 in (5 cm) squares

1 aubergine, cubed, salted, pressed for 30 minutes, rinsed and cut into 2 in (5 cm) pieces *or* 6 oz (175 g) beancurd, pressed, shallow fried in a little oil and cut into 2 in (5 cm) pieces

2 tablespoons (30 ml) vegetable oil
2 tablespoons miso
2 tablespoons sugar
4 tablespoons (60 ml) soya sauce
¼ teaspoon cayenne pepper

Preheat the grill on its medium setting or prepare glowing charcoal on a barbecue. Divide the mixed vegetables into 4 equal portions and arrange them in colourful patterns on 4 skewers. Brush the vegetables with oil. Combine the miso, sugar, soya sauce and cayenne and mix well together. Grill the vegetables until lightly browned all over. Remove them from the grill and liberally brush with the miso mixture. Return to the grill and cook, turning as necessary, for another 2–3 minutes. Serve immediately.

Mixed Vegetable Salad with Coconut Sauce — Serves 4

In Indonesia this dish is called urap. It can be made with any combination of vegetables, cooked or raw. If the vegetables are cooked they should be either lightly steamed or parboiled, so that their full colour and texture are retained.

2 cloves garlic
1 medium onion, chopped
1–2 fresh *or* dried red chillies
6 oz (175 g) desiccated coconut
4 fl oz (100 ml) water
1 teaspoon brown sugar
salt to taste
1 lb (450 g) total weight of one or more types of lightly cooked or raw vegetables, chopped, shredded or sliced. The following are suggestions only:

aubergines, cubed, rinsed, drained and steamed until tender
carrots, sliced and parboiled *or* raw and grated
courgettes, sliced
cucumber, peeled, seeded and diced
green or French beans, stringed, chopped and parboiled
green *or* red peppers, seeded and cut into strips, raw *or* parboiled

Put the garlic, onion and chillies into a blender and blend the mixture to a smooth paste. Put the coconut in a bowl, stir in the water and sugar, and add salt to taste. Mix in the spice paste. Stand the bowl on another upturned bowl in a pan containing about 1 in (2.5 cm) of water. Boil the water and steam the coconut sauce for 20 minutes. Meanwhile, prepare your vegetables and combine them into a salad. Toss the salad in a hot or cold sauce and serve. Hot sauce is normally best with cooked vegetables, and cold sauce with raw vegetables.

Green Salad with Coconut Sauce

Prepare a green salad from a selection of vegetables in season, e.g. lettuce, cabbage, Chinese cabbage, watercress, spinach (lightly cooked), French or green beans (sliced and parboiled), young peas in their pods. Make the coconut sauce from the urap recipe above, chill it and toss the salad in it.

Hunan Vegetable Hotpot   *Serves 4*

China
You will need a very large cooking pot in which to cook the hotpot. Earthenware or porcelain-clad iron work well. If the pot is beautiful, bring it to the table and serve the meal from it in large soup plates. Almost any ingredients can go into a hotpot: let your imagination and available foods guide you.

- 2 pints (1.1 litres) clear vegetable stock
- 4 oz (100 g) cauliflower, cut into florets
- 2 medium courgettes, sliced diagonally
- 2 medium red *or* yellow peppers, seeded and quartered
- 3 oz (75 g) spring onions, chopped
- 4 oz (100 g) mange-tout
- 4 oz (100 g) mushrooms, sliced
- 2 small carrots, sliced
- 2 small turnips, peeled and sliced
- salt to taste

Bring the stock to the boil in your best-looking large pot. Add to it a selection of light-coloured, tender vegetables such as those above. Cook slowly until the vegetables are tender – about 15 minutes.

Broccoli with Coconut and Lemon Sauce

Serves 4 as a side dish

Indonesia

1 lb (450 g) broccoli	1 clove garlic, crushed
water	1 fresh *or* dried red chilli, chopped and seeded *or* ¼ teaspoon chilli powder
2 tablespoons (30 ml) vegetable oil	
4 oz (100 g) desiccated *or* freshly grated coconut	juice of 1 lemon
	3 tablespoons (45 ml) water
½ medium onion, sliced	salt to taste

Remove any large leaves from the broccoli, cut off the stem ends and divide any large heads into florets. Place the broccoli in a saucepan, add ½ in (1 cm) water, add salt, cover and cook gently until tender (10–15 minutes). Meanwhile, heat the oil in a frying pan and add the coconut, onion, garlic and chilli. Stir fry until the coconut is browned and the onion is softened. Put the mixture into a blender, add the lemon juice, water and more salt if needed and blend it to a smooth sauce. Drain the broccoli, pour the coconut and lemon sauce over it and serve.

Cos Lettuce in Cream Sauce

Serves 3

Cream sauces in Chinese cooking are fairly rare. Any lettuce can be used in this delicately flavoured dish.

1 good head cos lettuce	½ oz (15 g) cornflour
4 fl oz (100 ml) milk	2 fl oz (50 ml) peanut oil
salt to taste	½ teaspoon sugar
4 fl oz (100 ml) stock	1 tablespoon butter

Cut out and discard the lettuce core. Separate the lettuce leaves. Keep the small leaves whole and chop the larger ones into 4 in (10 cm) lengths. Rinse and drain well, then pat dry. Combine the milk, salt and vegetable stock and set aside. Put the cornflour into a bowl, add about 3 tablespoons (45 ml) of the milk and stock mixture and set aside. In a wok or frying pan heat 3 tablespoons (45 ml) of the oil. When it is hot take the pan off the heat, add the lettuce and then turn the heat to high, cooking, turning and stirring the lettuce for about 1 minute. Add the sugar and more salt to taste if necessary. Cook for about 3 minutes, then with a slotted spoon quickly transfer the lettuce to a serving dish. Wipe out the pan. Heat the remainder of the oil in the pan and add the milk and stock mixture and the cornflour mixture. Bring to the boil, stirring. When thickened, turn off the heat and stir in the butter. Add more salt if necessary. Spoon the sauce over the lettuce and serve immediately.

Thai Curried Beancurd with Vegetables   *Serves 4*

The vegetables given in this recipe are only suggestions and any suitable combination available may be used. This recipe, unlike most Thai curries, does not use coconut milk and it is a little quicker and that much more simple to prepare. Serve with rice.

3 tablespoons (45 ml) vegetable oil
2 tablespoons curry powder mixed to a paste with 2 tablespoons (30 ml) white vinegar and 2 tablespoons (30 ml) water
8 oz (225 g) beancurd, pressed and cut into 1 in (2.5 cm) cubes
2 tablespoons (30 ml) soya sauce
1 teaspoon grated lemon rind *or* chopped lemon grass

4 oz (100 g) green beans, cut into 2 in (5 cm) lengths
4 oz (100 g) cauliflower, cut into florets
4 oz (100 g) cabbage *or* Chinese cabbage, coarsely shredded
4 oz (100 g) fresh mushrooms, sliced
2 teaspoons sugar
garnish
finely chopped coriander *or* mint *or* parsley leaves

Heat the oil in a large pan or wok and stir fry the curry paste for 3–4 minutes. Add the beancurd, soya sauce and lemon rind and continue to stir fry for a further 6–7 minutes. Add the green beans, cauliflower, cabbage and mushrooms. Cook, stirring, until they are tender enough to eat but still retain some 'bite' (about 4–5 minutes). Stir in the sugar and serve garnished with fresh herbs.

Stir Fried Vegetables   *Serves 4*

This South East Asian recipe can be used for a single vegetable or a combination. If using more than one vegetable, add to the pan first those that take longest to cook.

2 tablespoons (30 ml) vegetable oil
1 clove garlic, crushed
1 small onion, finely sliced
2 bay leaves *or* daun salem leaves
1 teaspoon grated lemon peel *or* 1 stalk lemon grass, chopped
1 lb (450 g) total weight washed and chopped vegetables. Select one or more from:

beansprouts
cabbage, shredded
carrots, sliced
celery, chopped
courgettes, sliced
French *or* green beans, stringed and chopped
green *or* red peppers, seeded, cored and sliced
2 teaspoons (10 ml) dark soya sauce
salt to taste

Heat the oil in a wok or frying pan and add the garlic, onion, bay leaves and lemon peel. Stir fry the mixture until the onion is softened. Add the vegetables (hardest first) and stir fry until they are lightly cooked but still crunchy. Add soya sauce and then, if necessary, salt to taste. Stir well and serve.

Variation
For chilli hot vegetables add 1–2 fresh or dried chillies, finely chopped with the garlic, onion and other spices. Raw peanuts (4 oz/100 g) are also good fried along with the vegetables.

Yellow and Green Summer Vegetables — *Serves 4*

China

1 tablespoon (15 ml) oil
2 large courgettes, sliced diagonally into 1 in (2 cm) chunks
2 small yellow pumpkins *or* marrows, diced diagonally into 1 in (2 cm) chunks

1 tablespoon grated onion
1 teaspoon (5 ml) soya sauce
freshly milled black pepper

Heat the oil in a heavy pan with a tight-fitting lid. Add the courgettes and pumpkin and stir well to coat all the pieces with oil. Cook over a high heat long enough for steam to begin rising from the vegetables, then cover and reduce the heat as much as possible. Cook for 8 minutes, shaking the pan occasionally to prevent sticking. Check the courgettes and marrows – they should be just beginning to go tender. Add the onion and soya sauce and cover again. Simmer until the vegetables are tender but still retain some 'bite'. Serve at once, sprinkled with coarse black pepper.

Honey Glazed Mushrooms   Serves 4

China
Serve hot or cold as an accompaniment to other dishes.

1 lb (450 g) fresh young mushrooms	1 tablespoon (15 ml) clear honey
1 tablespoon (15 ml) peanut oil	2 tablespoons (30 ml) soya sauce

Wipe the mushrooms clean and trim the stalks level with the caps. Heat the oil in a wok or frying pan and swirl it around to coat the pan evenly. Add the mushrooms and stir fry for 1 minute over a medium high heat. Add the honey and soya sauce, turn the heat low, cover and cook for about 3 minutes. Uncover and cook until the liquid thickens, turning the mushrooms in the honey and soya mixture to coat them.

Rice Dishes (Including Sushi)

Rice is an essential part of every meal in the Far East. In Japan the word for rice, *han*, is even given the honourable prefix *go* and is referred to as *go-han*. The first clear written record of rice dates to 2800 BC during the reign of the Chinese Emperor Chin-Nung, who is said to have given rice its name. Since even before that time rice has been the staple food of the peoples of South East Asia, the humid, sub-tropical regions of these areas providing some of the best rice-growing environments in the world. However, even in optimum conditions rice is still a labour-intensive crop and the arduous, back-breaking work involved in its cultivation has imposed a tough regime on the lives of the peasants who grow it. This in turn has influenced the cultural outlook and customs of the Far East.

Many varieties of rice are grown in the Far East but they can broadly be divided into long grain and short grain rices. Long grain rices remain in separate grains and become light and fluffy when cooked. Short grain rices are soft when cooked, and the cooked grains stick gently to one another. For savoury dishes, except in Japan and parts of China, long grain rice is usually favoured. Almost without exception white polished rice is preferred to brown rice, even though the latter is more nutritious. Short grain rice is used for desserts, the sticky, glutinous varieties being the most popular. In the West pudding rice is a substitute for sticky rice.

The recipes given here are divided into simple rice dishes, fried rice dishes, sushi rice and other main meal rice dishes.

Simple Rice Dishes

Plain Boiled Rice

Red Rice

Green Rice

Chestnut Rice

Yellow Rice with Coconut Milk

Yellow Rice with Spices

Sweet Smelling Coconut Rice

Spiced Rice

Mushrooms and Rice

Rice and Beansprouts

Fried Rice Dishes

Thai Fried Rice

Rice Stuffed Pineapple

Japanese Fried Rice

Chinese Fried Rice with Mixed Vegetables

Thai Fried Curried Rice

Beancurd and Broccoli Fried Rice

Combination Fried Rice

Sushi Rice Dishes

Sushi Rice

Nigiri Sushi

Chira Sushi

Norimaki Sushi

Rice Dishes (Including Sushi)

Main Rice Dishes

Vegetable Donburi

Tempura Donburi

Hot Green Vegetable Rice

Festive Rice Cone

Simple Rice Dishes

Plain Boiled Rice *Serves 4–6*

Each of the countries in the Far East has its own favourite methods of cooking rice but essentially all the methods are very similar and I am only giving one basic, general set of instructions here. The recipe is for loose white rice only. If you buy packaged rice follow the instructions given on the packet.

1 lb (450 g) long grain rice salt (optional)
2 volumes water to 1
  volume rice (slightly less
  water for short grain rice)

Measure the rice by cupfuls into a sieve or colander and rinse it under cold water until the water runs clear. Drain the rice and transfer it to a heavy-bottomed pan with a tight-fitting lid. (You can improve the fit of a lid by wrapping it in aluminium foil.) Add 2 volumes more water than rice, and salt if it is being used. Cover the pan and bring the rice to the boil over a high heat. Stir the rice with the handle end of a wooden spoon, then cover it again, reduce the heat to very low and leave it to simmer for 15–20 minutes. At this stage the rice should just be tender. Don't lift the lid off to check, or you will loose some of the steam; the timing has to be guessed at first. Remove the pan from the heat and leave it to stand, still covered, for 5 minutes. The rice is ready to be served when all the water has been absorbed. Fluff it up with a wooden spoon just before serving.

Red Rice   Serves 4

This Japanese dish is usually made from a variety of Japanese rice called mochi, which is sweeter than the regular kind. Red Rice is known as sekihan when made with mochi, and is a great favourite for festive occasions, especially Hina Matouri or Girls' Day. A red colouring is given to the rice by cooking it with aduki beans. Mochi rice is not readily available in the West, and the recipe given here is for regular rice. If you cannot obtain aduki beans, use red or kidney beans instead. Rice and aduki beans eaten together provide a rich source of protein as well as a colourful dish.

4 oz (100 g) aduki or kidney beans, soaked in water for 6 hours or more
2 pints (1.1 litres) water
1 lb (450 g) rice, washed and drained

garnish
1 teaspoon salt
2 tablespoons sesame seeds, toasted

Drain the soaked beans. Place in a pan with the water, bring to the boil, reduce the heat, cover and simmer until cooked (about 1½ hours). Drain and reserve the liquid. Put the rice in the pan, add the bean cooking liquid plus, if necessary, enough water to make the volume up to 1½ pints (825 ml). Cover and bring to the boil. Add the cooked beans, stir, cover, reduce the heat and simmer until the rice is cooked (about 15–20 minutes). Combine the salt and toasted sesame seeds. Serve Red Rice hot or cold, garnished with a sesame seed and salt mixture (called gomashio).

Green Rice   Serves 4–6

Japan

1 lb (450 g) rice, washed and drained
2 volumes water to 1 volume of rice

8 oz (225 g) spinach, washed and drained *or* 1 large bunch watercress, washed and drained
salt to taste

Cook the rice by the basic method. Meanwhile prepare the greens and blanch them briefly in a pan of boiling water. As soon as the leaves soften, rinse them under cold water. Drain well and gently press out as much moisture as you can. Chop the greens into shreds, add salt to taste and stir them into the cooked rice. Serve.

Chestnut Rice   Serves 4–6

Japan

15–20 fresh chestnuts
2 tablespoons (30 ml) soya sauce
2 tablespoons (30 ml) sake *or* medium sweet white wine
1 lb (450 g) rice, washed and drained
2 volumes water to 1 volume rice
garnish
1 tablespoon sesame seeds, dry roasted

With a sharp knife make a criss-cross incision in the shells of the chestnuts and boil them in water for 5 minutes. Drain the chestnuts, rinse them under cold water, peel them and cut into quarters. Combine the chestnuts, soya sauce, sake, rice and water and cook by the basic method. Serve sprinkled with roasted sesame seeds.

Yellow Rice with Coconut Milk   Serves 4–6

In this Indonesian recipe the rice is coloured yellow with turmeric and cooked in coconut milk instead of water. The finished rice should be colourfully garnished. It makes a bright, rich centrepiece to a special meal. For yellow rice cooked without coconut milk see the next recipe.

1 lb (450 g) long grain rice, washed and drained
1 pint (550 ml) medium coconut milk
1 teaspoon ground turmeric
1 bay leaf *or* daun salem leaf
½ teaspoon salt

garnish
choose from:
onion flakes, fried brown
finely sliced cucumber
fresh chillies, seeded and chopped

Put the rice in a bowl, cover it with water and leave it to soak for 2–3 hours. Drain it and then put the rice with the other ingredients into a heavy-bottomed pan. Bring the rice to a gentle boil and cook it over a low heat, uncovered, until all the coconut milk has been absorbed. Now stir the rice with the handle end of a wooden spoon and then cover the pot with a tight-fitting lid. Reduce the heat to the lowest setting possible and gently cook the rice for another 15 minutes. The rice is now ready to tip into a serving bowl, garnish and serve.

Yellow Rice with Spices

Serves 4–6

Indonesia

- 1 lb (450 g) long grain rice, washed and drained
- 2 tablespoons (30 ml) vegetable oil
- 1 small onion, finely diced
- 1 teaspoon ground turmeric
- 1 teaspoon ground coriander
- ½ teaspoon ground cumin
- ½ teaspoon ground cinnamon
- salt to taste
- 1 pint (550 ml) water, boiling

Put the rice in a bowl, cover it with cold water and leave it to soak for 2–3 hours. Drain it, then set the rice aside. Heat the vegetable oil in a heavy-bottomed pan and stir fry the onion in it until softened. Add the spices and salt and sauté the mixture for another minute. Stir the rice into the pan and sauté the rice and spices for 2–3 minutes. Pour in the boiling water and cook the rice over a moderate heat until the water is absorbed. Stir the rice with the handle end of a wooden spoon and cover the pot with a tight-fitting lid. Reduce the heat to very low, cook the rice gently for another 15 minutes and then serve.

Sweet Smelling Coconut Rice

Serves 4–6

This delicious South East Asian rice dish is simple to prepare and it gives an exotic aroma to even the simplest meal.

- 1¼ pints (700 ml) medium coconut milk
- 1½ teaspoons salt
- ¼ teaspoon freshly ground black pepper
- ¼ teaspoon ground cloves
- ½ teaspoon ground nutmeg
- ½ teaspoon ground cinnamon
- 1 teaspoon grated lemon rind *or* chopped lemon grass
- 1 bay leaf *or* daun salem leaf
- 1 lb (450 g) long grain rice, washed and drained

Put all the ingredients except the rice into a heavy saucepan and bring the mixture to a gentle boil, stirring constantly. Add the rice and bring back to a very slow boil, stirring. Cover the pan with a tight-fitting lid, reduce the heat and simmer for 20 minutes. Remove the pan from the heat, stir and then set aside, off the heat, for 5 minutes before serving.

Spiced Rice
Serves 4–6

The Indonesian name for this dish, nasi gemuk, means rice cooked in oil, and in this recipe the spices are fried in oil, the raw rice is stirred in, and then water or coconut milk are added and the mixture simmered until the rice is cooked.

3 tablespoons (45 ml) vegetable oil
1 in (2.5 cm) piece of cinnamon
1 clove
2 cardamom pods, broken open
1 small onion, finely diced
2 cloves garlic, crushed
½ in (1 cm) piece root ginger, finely chopped
½ teaspoon ground coriander
1 lb (450 g) long grain rice, washed and drained
salt to taste
1¼ pints (700 ml) water *or* stock *or* coconut milk

Heat the oil in a heavy saucepan or wok and add the cinnamon, clove and cardamoms. Fry for 1–2 minutes. Add the onion, garlic, root ginger and coriander and stir fry for another 1–2 minutes. Stir the rice into the spice mixture. Add salt to taste. Carefully pour in the water, stock or coconut milk (traditionally used) and bring the rice to the boil. Cover, reduce the heat and simmer the rice for 15–20 minutes or until it is tender.

Variation
If you like chilli hot dishes, add 1–2 finely chopped chillies along with the onion and garlic.

Mushrooms and Rice
Serves 4–6

For this Japanese recipe shiitake or dried mushrooms are traditionally used, but fresh mushrooms may be substituted or Chinese dried black mushrooms.

1 lb (450 g) rice, washed and drained
2 volumes water to 1 volume rice
4 shiitake *or* Chinese dried black mushrooms, soaked in warm water for 30 minutes, drained, stems discarded and caps sliced *or* 6 oz (175 g) fresh mushrooms, thinly sliced
1 tablespoon (15 ml) soya sauce
½ teaspoon salt
2 tablespoons (30 ml) water

Cook the rice by the basic method. Meanwhile heat the oil in a small pan and lightly sauté the mushrooms until just softened. Add the soya sauce, salt and water. Cover the pan and simmer very gently for 5 minutes. Remove the lid and reduce the liquid by gentle simmering until the mushrooms are only just moist. Combine the hot, cooked rice and mushrooms, cover, leave to stand for 5 minutes and then serve.

Rice and Beansprouts *Serves 4–6*

China

1 lb (450 g) rice, washed and drained
2 volumes water to 1 volume rice
1 tablespoon (15 ml) vegetable oil (sesame oil for preference)
1 clove garlic, finely chopped
½ medium onion, finely chopped
1½ tablespoons sesame paste *or* tahini
6 oz (175 g) beansprouts
2 tablespoons (30 ml) soya sauce

Cook the rice by the basic method. Meanwhile, heat the oil in a wok or frying pan and sauté the garlic and onion until golden. Stir in the sesame paste and then the beansprouts. Stir fry until the beansprouts are very hot. Stir the mixture and the soya sauce into the hot cooked rice and serve.

Fried Rice Dishes

Fried rice is quick to make and the method is open to any number of variations from the very basic to the most elaborate. The following recipes come from various countries in the Far East but the basic method is the same for each of them. Cooked rice is fried with flavourings and a combination of other ingredients. The recipes given here can be adapted to suit the particular ingredients you have available, and your own taste.

Boiled rice used in the preparation of fried rice dishes is best made a couple of hours beforehand (or use leftover rice from the day before). If it is soggy or overcooked the fried rice will be sticky and too soft.

Thai Fried Rice

Serves 4

3 tablespoons (45 ml) vegetable oil
2 cloves garlic, finely chopped
1 medium onion, finely chopped
1 red *or* green pepper, seeded and chopped
1 in (2.5 cm) piece root ginger, peeled and cut into fine slivers (optional)
2 tablespoons (30 ml) soya sauce
1 lb (450 g) cooked rice
2 tablespoons (30 ml) tomato purée

garnish
1 small *or* ½ medium cucumber, sliced
2 tablespoons chopped coriander leaves

Heat the oil in a wok or large saucepan. Add the garlic and onion and fry until the onion is softened. Add the pepper and ginger, if used, and stir fry for 2 minutes. Add the soya sauce, stir well and then add the rice and tomato purée. Stir fry until the rice is well heated through. Transfer to a serving dish. Surround the edge of the plate with cucumber slices and garnish the rice with coriander leaves. Serve immediately.

Rice Stuffed Pineapple

Serves 4 as side dish

Cut the top off a large pineapple about one quarter of the way down. Scoop out all the flesh. Cut it into cubes and use 8 oz (225 g) in the Thai Fried Rice recipe above (add the pineapple with the pepper and ginger). Preheat the oven to 350°F (180°C, gas mark 4). Stuff the hollowed out pineapple with the fried rice, put the top back on and bake it for 15 minutes.

Japanese Fried Rice

Serves 4

2 tablespoons (30 ml) vegetable oil
1 clove garlic, crushed
1 medium onion, diced
4 oz (100 g) mushrooms, sliced
4 oz (100 g) celery *or* French beans, chopped
1 lb (450 g) cooked rice
6 oz (175 g) pressed beancurd, cut into 1 in (2.5 cm) cubes (optional)
1 egg *or* 1-egg omelette cut into strips
2 tablespoons (30 ml) soya sauce

Heat the oil in a heavy frying pan. Add the crushed garlic and onion. Sauté until the onions are just soft, and then add the mushrooms and celery. Fry gently for 2–3 minutes, retaining the texture of each vegetable. Stir in the rice and beancurd. Heat through, stirring constantly. Break the egg over the rice mixture, sprinkle on the soya sauce and mix well. Alternatively, for a fried rice with a less creamy texture, replace the egg with strips of omelette.

Chinese Fried Rice with Mixed Vegetables   *Serves 6*

1 lb (450 g) white rice, washed and drained
1¼ pints (700 ml) water
12 Chinese dried mushrooms
1–2 large leeks
4 oz (100 g) fresh beansprouts
3 tablespoons (45 ml) peanut oil
1 tablespoon (15 ml) sesame oil
1 teaspoon (5 ml) finely grated fresh root ginger
1 teaspoon (5 ml) finely grated garlic
8 oz (225 g) green beans, stringed and thinly sliced
4 stalks celery, thinly sliced
2 medium carrots, coarsely grated
1 piece canned bamboo shoot, cut into matchsticks
4 oz (100 g) spring onions, finely sliced
4 fl oz (100 ml) mushroom liquid
2 tablespoons (30 ml) light soya sauce
salt to taste

Put rice and water into a heavy saucepan with a close-fitting lid and bring to the boil over a high heat. Then turn very low, cover the pan tightly and cook for 20 minutes. Turn the rice out of the pan, spread it on a large tray or baking dish and allow to cool. Refrigerate. This should be done some hours before the rice is to be fried, or even the day before.

Soak the mushrooms for 30 minutes in enough hot water to cover them, then squeeze out as much liquid as possible. Reserve the liquor. Cut off the stems with a sharp knife and discard them. Cut the caps into thin slices (if they are very large cut the slices in half). Wash the leeks well in cold water, making sure that all the grit between the leaves is washed away. Cut into thin slices, using all the white part and about 2–3 in (5–7 cm) of the green. Wash and drain the beansprouts and pinch off any straggly brown 'tails'. Heat the peanut oil and sesame oil in a large wok or frying pan, add the ginger and garlic and fry over medium heat, stirring well, for 30 seconds. Add the mushrooms, leeks, green beans, celery and carrots, and stir fry over high heat for 3 minutes. Add the beansprouts and bamboo shoots and fry for 1 minute longer.

Add the rice, toss and fry over high heat until the grains are heated through. Add the spring onions. Mix the mushroom liquid and the soya sauce together and sprinkle evenly over the rice. Continue stirring to mix well together, and season to taste with salt. Serve hot.

Thai Fried Curried Rice   Serves 6–8

3 tablespoons (45 ml) vegetable oil
1–2 tablespoons (15–30 ml) mild curry paste (shop bought)
8 oz (225 g) beancurd, drained, pressed and cut into 1 in (2.5 cm) cubes
8 oz (225 g) green beans, cut into 1 in (2.5 cm) lengths, blanched just tender in boiling water and drained

2 lb (900 g) cooked long grain rice (about 12 oz/350 g raw rice)
2 tablespoons finely chopped onion *or* shallot
1–2 red chillies, seeded and finely chopped (optional)
2 spring onions, finely chopped
1 tablespoon (15 ml) lemon *or* lime juice
1 tablespoon (15 ml) soya sauce

Heat the oil in a wok or large frying pan and stir fry the curry paste for 3–4 minutes. Add the beancurd and beans and stir fry until well heated through. Add the rice, mix well and continue to stir fry until heated through. Transfer to a serving dish or bowl. Sprinkle chopped onions over the top and chillies (if used). Finally, sprinkle with spring onions, lemon juice and soya sauce before serving.

Variation
Replace the cooked rice in the recipe above with cooked, drained egg noodles.

Beancurd and Broccoli Fried Rice   Serves 4–6

Thailand

3 tablespoons (45 ml) vegetable oil
2 cloves garlic, finely chopped
8 oz (225 g) broccoli, cut into bite-size pieces
6 oz (175 g) beancurd, pressed and cut into 1 in (2.5 cm) cubes
2 tablespoons (30 ml) soya sauce

½ teaspoon (2.5 ml) chilli sauce (optional)
1 lb (450 g) cooked rice
garnish
1 egg, beaten, fried as a thin omelette and cut into strips
2 tablespoons chopped coriander
1 tomato, cut into wedges
1 lemon, cut into wedges

Heat the oil in a wok or large saucepan, add the garlic and fry until golden. Add the broccoli and stir fry for 2 minutes. Add the beancurd and stir fry for a further 2 minutes. Stir into the pan the soya sauce, chilli sauce and then the rice. Stir fry until the rice is well heated through. Transfer to a large serving plate or bowl. Decorate the top with strips of omelette, coriander and wedges of tomato and lemon.

Variations
1. For a chilli dish add to the frying garlic 2–4 fresh chillies, seeded and finely chopped. Omit the chilli sauce later.

2. For a curried dish, substitute 1 teaspoon curry powder for the chilli sauce.

Combination Fried Rice   *Serves 4–6*

Thailand
Combination fried rice is useful as a one-dish meal, or it can be served as part of a more elaborate dinner party.

2 fl oz (50 ml) vegetable oil
2 medium onions, finely chopped
2 cloves garlic, finely chopped
1–2 red chillies, seeded and finely chopped
1 green pepper, seeded and cut into thin strips
3 oz (75 g) beansprouts, washed and drained
2 medium tomatoes, quartered
3 eggs, lightly beaten
1½ lb (700 g) cooked rice
2 tablespoons (30 ml) soya sauce
3 tablespoons (45 ml) tomato ketchup (tomato ketchup is a popular ingredient in Thai cookery. Use tomato purée if you prefer)
1 teaspoon salt

garnish
4 spring onions, chopped
2 tablespoons chopped coriander leaves
1 lemon *or* lime, cut into wedges

Heat the oil in a wok or large saucepan. Add the onion, garlic, chillies and green pepper and fry until the onion is softened. Add the beansprouts and tomatoes and stir fry for 2–3 minutes. Pour the beaten eggs into the middle of this mixture and stir fry until they are well combined. Stir in the rice, soya sauce, tomato ketchup and salt. Stir fry until the rice is heated through and all the ingredients are well mixed (about 5 minutes). Transfer to a large plate or bowl, garnish with spring onions, coriander leaves and lemon wedges, and serve at once.

Variation
Fry with the onion, garlic and chilli a 1 in (2.5 cm) piece of root ginger, cut into fine slices.

Sushi Rice Dishes

Sushi is a generic term used to describe a variety of Japanese dishes in which the basic ingredient is cooked rice seasoned with rice vinegar and sugar.

Nigiri Sushi is perhaps the most popular, and in this the sushi rice is formed into different shapes which are then topped with a selection of garnishes.

Chira Sushi is a rice salad made with sushi rice. It is substantial, and may be used as a main course or salad dish.

Norimaki Sushi is made by wrapping sushi rice and other ingredients in thin sheets of nori seaweed. The resulting Swiss roll shape is cut into thick slices crosswise, and each piece displays the colourful filling.

The recipe for sushi rice is given first, followed by recipes for the three types of sushi described above. There are of course many other types of sushi not discussed here, and if you want to read more on the subject see *Japanese Cooking* by Shizuo Tsuji (Kodansha International, 1980).

Sushi Rice

12 oz (350 g) white short grain rice
1 pint (550 ml) water
4 tablespoons (60 ml) rice vinegar *or* cider vinegar

3 tablespoons white sugar
½ teaspoon salt

Place the rice in a heavy pan. Add the water, cover the pan and bring to the boil quickly. Turn the heat right down and allow the pan to simmer for 15 minutes. Turn off the heat and allow the rice to stand for 5–10 minutes. Put the rice in a non-metallic bowl and set aside.

Combine the vinegar, sugar and salt and bring the mixture to the boil, stirring. Pour this dressing over the hot rice. Turn the mixture gently with a wet wooden spoon in one hand while with the other hand fan the rice with a flat pan lid or rolled-up newspaper. This cools the rice quickly and gives it an authentic shine. Set the rice aside.

Nigiri Sushi   Serves 4–6

Prepare sushi rice by the basic method above, and while it is still warm prepare the rice shapes as follows. Wet your hands and, using 1 heaped tablespoon of sushi rice, form an oval, ball or square shape. Continue until all the rice is used up. Wet your hands as necessary to prevent the rice sticking. Arrange the rice shapes on a serving dish and garnish with one or more of the following:
1. A thin 1-egg omelette, cut into strips and brushed with soya sauce.
2. Thin slices of cucumber spread sparingly with English mustard or Japanese wasabi.
3. Sesame seeds, lightly dry roasted.
4. Thinly sliced mushrooms, lightly cooked in equal parts of soya sauce and sugar.
5. Nori seaweed, toasted and crumbled.
6. Parboiled and drained vegetables – e.g. carrots, French beans, celery or green peppers – cut into small portions.

Chira Sushi   Serves 4

3 tablespoons (45 ml) vegetable oil
sushi rice, prepared as above
1 egg, beaten
1 tablespoon (15 ml) soya sauce
1 medium carrot, peeled and sliced into thin rounds
1 medium onion, finely diced
1 stick celery, finely chopped
2 oz (50 g) mushrooms, quartered
garnish
2 teaspoons (10 ml) finely sliced pickled ginger (optional)

Brush a large frying pan with a little of the oil. Beat the egg with 1 teaspoon (5 ml) of the soya sauce and prepare a thin omelette in the frying pan. Remove the omelette and cut it into thin strips. Set them aside.

In the same pan heat two-thirds of the remaining oil and sauté the carrot, onion and celery for 2–3 minutes. Set them aside. Heat the remaining oil in the pan and sauté the mushrooms for a few minutes until just cooked. Remove them from the heat and stir in the remaining soya sauce.

Gently mix the sushi rice with the cooked vegetables and mushrooms in sauce. Transfer the mixture to a serving dish and mould it into a mound. Garnish the top with strips of omelette and pickled ginger. Serve at room temperature or chilled.

Norimaki Sushi   Serves 4

Norimaki Sushi traditionally has 6 different fillings, but 3 or 4 are usually enough. Below are suggestions for 8 fillings. Prepare however many you wish, and then proceed to assemble the Norimaki Sushi. If nori sheets are unavailable replace them with 4 thin omelettes cut into 8 × 8 in (20 × 20 cm) squares. They make a fine substitute.

Basic Ingredients

sushi rice prepared as above
4 sheets nori seaweed *or*
    omelette squares
3 or 4 of the following fillings:

Carrot Filling

1 medium carrot, quartered lengthwise and cut into sticks ¼ in (0.5 cm) thick
1 tablespoon (15 ml) vegetable oil
1 tablespoon (15 ml) water
pinch salt

Sauté the carrot sticks in oil for 2 minutes. Add water and salt. Simmer until the carrots are just soft.

Lotus Root Filling

1 medium can lotus roots, quartered lengthwise and cut into sticks ¼ in (0.5 cm) thick
1 tablespoon (15 ml) soya sauce
1 tablespoon (15 ml) water

Combine the ingredients and heat through.

Spinach Filling

4 oz (100 g) spinach leaves, washed and drained

1 tablespoon sesame seeds, toasted

salt to taste

Boil the spinach lightly in salted water for 2–3 minutes. Drain, press out excess water, chop and mix with the sesame seeds. Season to taste with salt.

French Bean Filling

4 oz (100 g) French beans, topped and tailed

water to cover

pinch salt

Cover the beans with water, bring to the boil and add salt. Simmer for 3–4 minutes. Drain and store in cold water.

Egg Filling (for nori only)

2 eggs, beaten

Prepare paper-thin omelettes and cut into ¼ in (0.5 cm) strips.

Mushroom Filling

4 oz (100 g) mushrooms, thinly sliced

4 tablespoons (60 ml) water

2 teaspoons sugar

2 teaspoons (10 ml) soya sauce

Simmer the mushrooms in the water, sugar and soya sauce until tender.

Watercress Filling

½ bunch watercress, washed, drained and cut into sprigs

Cucumber Filling

½ medium cucumber, peeled and cut into ¼ in (0.5 cm) strips

wasabi *or* English mustard to taste

Dab the cucumber strips sparingly with mustard or wasabi before laying them in Norimaki.

The above suggestions can be supplemented with your own ideas. Make full use of left-over cooked vegetables.

To assemble Norimaki Sushi

Hold individual sheets of nori seaweed over a direct heat source to crispen it. Place one on a bamboo table mat approximately 8 × 8 in (20 × 20 cm) or a damp cloth of the same size (a damp cloth makes the wrapping process a little more difficult, but not insurmountable). Divide the rice into 4 portions and spread one portion over the sheet of nori, leaving a 1 in (2.5 cm) gap at the top and bottom ends to allow for overlap. Lay the fillings in horizontal rows down the middle of the rice. Slightly moisten the exposed edges of the nori and then roll up the mixture in the mat or cloth. Make sure the ingredients are tightly encased by the seaweed and then unroll carefully. Trim the ends and cut the roll into 1 in (2.5 cm) thick slices.

Main Rice Dishes

Vegetable Donburi *Serves 4–6*

Donburi is a Japanese dish in which a bowl of boiled rice is served topped with a variety of cooked foods.

1 lb (450 g) rice, washed and drained	4 leaves spinach, chopped
2 tablespoons (30 ml) vegetable oil	4 oz (100 g) mushrooms, sliced
2 small leeks *or* 2 spring onions, thinly sliced	2 tablespoons (30 ml) soya sauce
1 medium carrot, grated	2 teaspoons sugar
2 sticks celery, chopped	salt to taste
	2 eggs, beaten
	black pepper to taste

Cook the rice by the basic method. Meanwhile, heat the oil in a heavy pan and sauté the vegetables and mushrooms until just soft. Add the soya sauce, sugar and salt to taste. Pour the beaten eggs over the mixture, add a pinch of black pepper, stir and cook until the eggs are just set. Put the cooked rice in a serving bowl, top with the egg and vegetable mixture, and serve.

Tempura Donburi

Tendon, an abbreviation of tempura (batter-coated foods, deep fried) and donburi, is the name used for this dish, which is a bed of rice topped with tempura. Recipes for tempura are given later.

Hot Green Vegetable Rice

Serves 4–6

China

2 tablespoons (30 ml) vegetable oil
2 leeks sliced
1 in (2.5 cm) root ginger, grated
1 clove garlic, sliced
1 green chilli, seeded and cut into strips

8 oz (225 g) long grain rice
boiling water
8 oz (225 g) spring greens, finely chopped
4 oz (100 g) mange-tout, sliced diagonally

Heat the oil in a frying pan or wok, add the leeks, ginger, garlic and green chilli, and fry quickly for 30 seconds. Add the rice, turning and stirring to coat each grain with the oil. Add sufficient boiling water just to cover the rice. Bring to the boil, cover and simmer for 5 minutes. Add the spring greens and the mange-tout, bring back to the boil and simmer for a further 7–9 minutes or until the rice is just tender. Drain and serve immediately.

Festive Rice Cone

Serves 8

One of the dishes always seen at an Indonesian celebration or festivity is a conical mound of yellow rice beautifully decorated with a variety of foods. Here is a recipe for the rice cone and some suggestions for garnishes. The quantities given will make rice for up to 8 people, and the recipe is excellent as a party dish.

2 tablespoons (30 ml) vegetable oil
1 large onion, finely diced
2 cloves garlic, crushed
2 lb (900 g) long grain white rice, washed and drained
1½ pints (825 ml) water
1½ pints (825 ml) fresh *or* canned coconut milk
1 teaspoon grated lemon rind *or* chopped lemon grass
4 bay leaves *or* daun salem leaves
2 teaspoons ground turmeric
3 teaspoons salt

garnish
select from:
fresh red chillies, cut into flower shapes (see method below)
fresh green chillies, seeded and cut into strips
boiled eggs, sliced
strips of omelette
roasted peanuts
cucumber slices
salad vegetables, chopped *or* shredded

Rice Dishes (Including Sushi) 111

Heat the oil in a heavy saucepan and sauté the onion and garlic until golden. Add the rice and stir it over the heat for a couple of minutes. Slowly pour in the water and then the coconut milk. Mix well and add the lemon rind, bay leaves, turmeric and salt. Bring the rice to the boil slowly, stirring constantly. Cover the pan with a tight-fitting lid and gently simmer for 20 minutes. Remove the pan from the heat, stir the contents and then set the pan aside, off the heat, for 5 minutes. The rice is now ready. Arrange it in a cone shape (a conical sieve helps) on a serving dish and garnish.

Note To make chilli flowers, slit the chillies 2 or 3 times vertically from tip almost to stem. Drop them into iced water and the strips will curl.

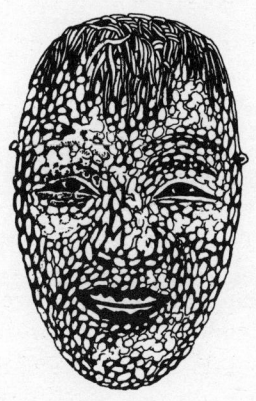

Noodle Dishes

Traditionally in the Far East flour has been used to prepare noodles and not, as in the West, to make bread. They are an important ingredient in Far Eastern cookery. Noodles are served in a variety of ways, but the most popular dishes are noodles in soup stock with garnishes or fried noodles with a combination of other ingredients. They are used in many different shapes and forms, but fall into four main categories.

Wheat flour noodles (called udon in Japan) are made from wheat flour, water and, for egg noodles, eggs. They are served boiled, stir fried and in soups.

Rice vermicelli noodles are made from rice flour and water. They are very thin and cook quickly. Rice vermicelli is normally soaked before use and then used in stir fry dishes and soups – although sometimes, as in the Thai dish mee krob, it is deep fried straight from the packet.

Rice flour noodles are a fatter version of rice vermicelli. They are sometimes available freshly made rather than dried. These noodles are served plain boiled, stir fried or in soups.

Finally, mung bean noodles, also called cellophane noodles, are made from mung bean flour and water. They are soaked before use in stir fried dishes or soups, or deep fried straight from the packet.

The Japanese also make a buckwheat flour noodle called soba, which is popular there but not found in the other countries of the Far East.

It is usually more convenient to buy noodles rather than make them (although recipes are given here for making the Japanese noodles soba and udon). Cooking instructions for noodles are, as a rule, given on the packets in which they are sold. It is most important to follow these carefully, since the success of a noodle recipe depends on the noodles not being over- or undercooked. Perfectly cooked noodles should be just soft on the outside, and just firm in the middle. Noodles which are to be fried are first boiled, after which it's important to drain, oil and air them before frying. This prevents them from overcooking in their own heat and keeps the texture firm, which is important for frying.

Fried Won-Tun

Egg Noodles in Vegetable Stock

Fried Noodles with Broccoli

Braised Noodles

Chinese Pancakes

Thai Fried Noodles

Noodles with Combination Topping

Thai Crisp Noodles

Cellophane Noodles, Egg and Vegetables

Cellophane Noodles in Hot Sauce with Broccoli

Japanese Noodles (Udon and Soba)

Udon or Soba in Soup Stock

Chinese Vegetables in Sauce with Plain Soft Fried Noodles

Casserole Noodles with Floating Eggs

Deep Fried Noodles (Yaki Soba)

Summer Noodles

Japanese Egg Noodles with Side Salad

Fried Won-Tun

Serves 4–6

Won-tun are small stuffed Chinese dumplings served either boiled in soups or, as in this recipe, deep fried. The pastry used to make the dumplings is very thin and may be bought ready-made from Chinese grocery stores. If you want to make your own a recipe is given. Serve fried won-tun as a starter or main meal dish. They may also be served with a sauce.

pastry

8 oz (225 g) plain flour
salt to taste
2 small eggs
water as required

} *or* 6 oz (175 g) won-tun skins

filling

8 oz (225 g) mushrooms, finely chopped	1 tablespoon (15 ml) soya sauce
2 spring onions, finely chopped	1 tablespoon (15 ml) vegetable oil
2 tablespoons finely chopped parsley	1 teaspoon cornflour
	salt and black pepper to taste
4–6 water chestnuts (tinned), finely chopped	

plus

oil for deep frying   1 egg white

To make the filling, combine and mix well all the filling ingredients.

To make the pastry, first sift the flour and salt into a mixing bowl. Beat the eggs into the flour and add enough water to form a firm but pliable dough. Knead well by hand or in a food processor for 5 minutes. Dust a board with flour and roll out a portion of the dough into as thin a sheet as possible. Cut this sheet into 4 in (10 cm) squares and set them aside. Repeat for all the dough. Alternatively, use shop-bought won-tun skins.

Place a tablespoon of filling onto a square of pastry and fold the corners over to make a triangle. Seal the edges by pressing hard with your fingers (use a little egg white to make a good joint if necessary) and repeat for all the filling and dough.

Heat the oil in a deep frying pan or wok and deep fry the won-tun a few at a time until crisp and golden brown (2–3 minutes). Drain and serve hot or at room temperature.

Egg Noodles in Vegetable Stock   Serves 4

This quick and filling dish is popular in Indonesia for a speedy lunchtime meal.

2 tablespoons (30 ml) oil	3 oz (75 g) beansprouts, washed
1 small onion, sliced	4 spring onions, chopped
2 cloves garlic, crushed	12 oz (350 g) noodles
2 pints (1.1 litres) vegetable stock	dark soya sauce to taste
1 in (2.5 cm) piece root ginger, finely chopped	*garnish*
salt and black pepper to taste	select from:
4 oz (100 g) cabbage leaves, shredded	sliced hard-boiled eggs
	thin strips of omelette
	tomato wedges
1–2 fresh *or* dried red chillies, finely chopped (optional)	chopped celery tops
	fried onion flakes *or* rings

Heat the oil in a large saucepan and add the onion and garlic. Stir fry until the onion is softened. Add the stock, ginger, salt and black pepper. Bring the mixture to the boil, reduce the heat, cover and simmer for 15 minutes. Add the cabbage leaves and chillies (if used), increase the heat and bring the mixture to a gentle boil. Add the beansprouts, spring onions and noodles. Loosen the strands of noodles with a fork, and stir in soya sauce to taste. Adjust the seasoning and simmer the soup, covered, for 5–7 minutes or until the noodles are cooked. Transfer the contents of the pan to a serving dish and garnish before serving.

Fried Noodles with Broccoli   Serves 4

The method described in this Indonesian recipe is a general one, and where I have given broccoli and celery as ingredients vegetables such as carrots, beansprouts, Chinese cabbage, mushrooms and so on may be substituted.

8 oz (225 g) noodles	4 spring onions, chopped
3 tablespoons (45 ml) oil	salt and black pepper to taste
1 medium onion, diced	*garnish*
2 cloves garlic, crushed	select from:
1 in (2.5 cm) piece root ginger, finely chopped	fried onion flakes
	1–2 fresh *or* dried red chillies, finely chopped
12 oz (350 g) broccoli, chopped	
3 sticks celery, chopped	fresh parsley, finely chopped
dark soya sauce to taste	thin omelette strips

Drop the noodles in lots of boiling water and cook them until they are just tender. Drain them and immediately toss them in 1 tablespoon (15 ml) oil; set them aside. Heat the remaining oil in a large, heavy frying pan or wok and fry the onion, garlic and ginger until the onion is softened. Add the broccoli and celery and stir fry for 2–3 minutes. Stir in the noodles, then stir fry them over a low heat for 2–3 minutes. Add the soya sauce and spring onions, season to taste with salt and pepper, and stir fry for another 1–2 minutes. Serve the fried noodles in individual bowls or a tureen, and garnish.

Braised Noodles   Serves 4

Fried noodles prepared as above are covered in hot soup stock, brought to the boil, garnished and served. Follow the fried noodle recipe to the point where the noodles are fried and ready to be removed from the frying pan. Now pour over them 8 fl oz (225 ml) hot vegetable soup stock. Bring to the boil, and boil for 1 minute before serving. Serve the braised noodles in individual bowls or a tureen, and garnish.

Chinese Pancakes   Makes 14

Serve these pancakes with savoury dishes. They make a nice change from rice or bread. See Egg Dishes chapter for Eggs on a Vegetable Nest, which is served with Chinese Pancakes.

8 oz (225 g) plain flour   1 tablespoon (15 ml) sesame oil
¾ pint (450 ml) boiling water

Put the flour into a bowl and pour the water into a well in the centre. Mix to a dough, then knead on a floured board until smooth and elastic. Divide into 14 portions. Roll each portion into a circle 4 in (10 cm) in diameter. Paint each thinly with sesame oil. Place one round on top of another and roll out the 'sandwich' to make a pancake 6 in (15 cm) in diameter. Make 6 more of these double pancakes.

Heat a large frying pan without oil on a low heat and fry the double pancakes, turning once so that each individual pancake is cooked on one side only. Keep shaking the pan to prevent the dough from sticking (do not use too high a heat). When cooked, separate each of the double pancakes to make 2 separate pancakes. Fold each single pancake into 4. Wrap in a warm cloth and keep warm until ready to serve.

Thai Fried Noodles   Serves 4

Thin rice noodles are soaked, drained, stir fried with beancurd and flavoured with tomato, lemon, garlic and soya sauce. This is not a chilli hot dish, but chilli sauce could be added if you wish.

- 12 oz (350 g) rice vermicelli
- 4 fl oz (100 ml) vegetable oil
- 2 cloves garlic, finely chopped
- 1 medium onion, finely chopped
- 8 oz (225 g) beancurd, pressed and cut into ½ in (1 cm) cubes
- 2 tablespoons (30 ml) tomato ketchup *or* tomato puree
- 2 teaspoons sugar
- 1 tablespoon (15 ml) soya sauce
- 2 tablespoons (30 ml) lemon juice *or* tamarind water
- 2 eggs, beaten
- 4 oz (100 g) beansprouts
- 2 tablespoons peanuts, coarsely ground *or* 1½ tablespoons crunchy peanut butter

garnish
- 2 tablespoons chopped coriander leaves
- 1 lemon cut into wedges
- 1 red chilli, seeded and thinly sliced (optional)

Put the rice noodles into a large bowl and just cover with very hot water, then set aside for 10 minutes. Drain, rinse with cold water and set aside again. Heat the oil in a large wok or saucepan and add the garlic and onion. Stir fry until the onion softens. Add the beancurd and heat through. Stir into the pan the tomato ketchup, sugar, soya sauce and lemon juice. Pour in the beaten eggs, give them 2–3 minutes to set and then stir them into the mixture. Add the noodles, half the beansprouts and all the crushed peanuts, mix well, toss and stir until the noodles are heated through. Turn onto a serving dish. Place the remaining beansprouts on one side of the noodles and then garnish the dish with coriander leaves, lemon wedges and chillies (if used). Serve immediately.

Variation
Replace the rice noodles with cooked egg noodles.

Noodles with Combination Topping   Serves 4–6

In this Thai dish the noodles are cooked separately and then served topped with a stir fried mixture of beancurd and Chinese mushrooms. It's very quick to prepare once the ingredients are marshalled together.

1 lb (450 g) rice noodles or 8 oz (225 g) egg noodles
4 tablespoons (60 ml) vegetable oil
2 cloves garlic, finely chopped
8 oz (225 g) beancurd, pressed and cut into ½ in (1 cm) cubes
1-egg omelette cut into strips
6 spring onions, finely chopped
6 Chinese dried mushrooms, soaked in hot water for 30 minutes, drained, stems discarded and caps sliced
2 tablespoons (30 ml) soya sauce

garnish
1 tablespoon chopped coriander leaves

Cook the noodles in plenty of salted boiling water until just tender (about 5 minutes for the rice noodles, 10–12 minutes for the egg noodles), drain immediately, and rinse in cold water until cooled to room temperature. Set aside. Heat the oil in a wok or large saucepan and add the garlic and beancurd. Stir fry for 2–3 minutes. Stir in the omelette strips, spring onions, mushroom slices and soya sauce and stir fry for 2 minutes. To reheat the noodles, pour boiling water over them in a colander. Drain the noodles and transfer them to a warmed serving dish. Pour over them the beancurd mixture and garnish with coriander leaves.

Thai Crisp Noodles   *Serves 4–6*

This dish, called mee krob, is a Thai speciality. Very fine rice vermicelli are first fried until crisp and then stir fried with a combination of vegetables, beansprouts and eggs in a sweet and sour sauce. Rice vermicelli is very brittle and flies everywhere when broken. To break it into small units ready for deep frying, put both your hands and the noodles inside a large plastic bag.

6 oz (175 g) rice vermicelli
vegetable oil for deep frying
1 medium onion, finely chopped
1–2 red chillies, seeded and finely chopped (optional)
3 cloves garlic, finely chopped
2 red or green peppers, seeded and cut into strips
4 oz (100 g) shredded Chinese cabbage or cabbage
1 medium bamboo shoot (tinned), chopped or 2 sticks celery, chopped
2 teaspoons grated lemon peel
2 tablespoons (30 ml) soya sauce
2 tablespoons (30 ml) rice vinegar or cider vinegar
2 tablespoons (30 ml) lemon juice
2 tablespoons sugar
4 eggs, beaten
4 oz (100 g) beansprouts

garnish
chopped coriander leaves

Heat the oil in a wok or deep frying pan and carefully drop in small handfuls of rice vermicelli. Fry them for just about 30 seconds and then turn them over and fry until golden brown and crisp. Remove them with a slotted spoon and repeat for all the noodles. Set them aside to drain on absorbent kitchen paper.

Pour the oil out of the wok or frying pan, leaving about 4 tablespoons (60 ml) behind. Fry the onion, chillies (if used) and garlic until softened, add the peppers, Chinese cabbage and bamboo shoots and stir fry for 3–4 minutes. In a bowl combine the lemon peel, soya sauce, vinegar, lemon juice and sugar. Add this mixture to the wok or pan and continue to simmer for a few minutes. Turn the heat up, make a hole in the middle of the ingredients and pour in the egg. Leave it to set a little and then stir it into the other ingredients until well set. Add the fried noodles and toss the mixture well to distribute all the ingredients evenly. Turn onto a serving dish, scatter beansprouts over the top, garnish with coriander leaves and serve.

Cellophane Noodles, Egg and Vegetables   Serves 4

Thailand

Cellophane or bean noodles are made from a puree of mung beans and water, strained, and then dried into sheets before pressing into noodles. They are hard and rubbery before soaking, but afterwards become soft and semi-transparent. In this recipe the noodles are soaked and then stir fried with beancurd, Chinese dried mushrooms and vegetables.

8 oz (225 g) cellophane noodles
3 tablespoons (45 ml) vegetable oil
3 cloves garlic, finely chopped
6 oz (175 g) beancurd, pressed and cut into 1 in (2.5 cm) cubes
6 Chinese dried mushrooms, soaked in warm water for 30 minutes, stems discarded and caps sliced
2 eggs
2 sticks celery, including leaves, finely chopped
2 spring onions, finely chopped
4 oz (100 g) beansprouts
1 tablespoon (15 ml) soya sauce
1 teaspoon freshly ground black pepper
garnish
2 oz (50 g) roasted peanuts, coarsely ground
coriander leaves

Soak the noodles in hot water for 3–4 minutes. Drain and cut them into 4 in (10 cm) lengths. Heat the oil in a wok or large frying pan and add the garlic. Fry until golden and then add the beancurd and chopped mushrooms. Heat through and stir in the noodles. Heat through again, stirring all the time, and then make a hole in the centre of the noodles. Break in the eggs and slowly stir them until just set. Now stir them into the noodles and add the celery, spring onions and beansprouts. Stir in the soya sauce and black pepper. Heat through again. Transfer to a serving dish, sprinkle the ground peanuts and coriander leaves over the top, and serve.

Cellophane Noodles in Hot Sauce with Broccoli   *Serves 4*

China

4 oz (100 g) cellophane noodles
1 tablespoon (15 ml) vegetable oil
6 spring onions, chopped
6 cloves garlic, chopped
1 lb (450 g) fresh broccoli spears, blanched
1 in (2.5 cm) fresh root ginger, finely chopped
1 teaspoon (5 ml) sesame oil
salt

hot sauce

¾ pint (400 ml) vegetable stock
½–1 tablespoon (10–15 ml) chilli sauce
1 tablespoon (15 ml) whole yellow bean sauce
½–1 dried red chilli, seeded and chopped *or* ½–1 teaspoon (2.5–5 ml) chilli powder
2 tablespoons (30 ml) light soya sauce

Soak the noodles in a large bowl of warm water for 15 minutes. When soft, drain them and throw away the water. Cut the noodles into 3 in (7.5 cm) lengths. Put the oil into a hot wok or frying pan. Then add the spring onions and garlic and stir fry quickly for a few seconds. Add the blanched broccoli spears and the ginger and stir fry for 5 minutes. If it seems dry add a little water. Remove from the heat.
   To prepare the hot sauce, mix all the sauce ingredients together

in a saucepan, bring to the boil, reduce the heat and cook over a gentle heat for 5 minutes. Return the vegetables to the heat and add the drained noodles and sesame oil. Cook over high heat for a further 5 minutes. Pour the hot sauce over the mixture and stir well. Ladle the noodles, vegetables and sauce into a large bowl and serve at once.

Japanese Noodles (Udon and Soba)

Udon is a fat noodle made from wheat flour (similar to spaghetti) and soba are buckwheat flour noodles. Soba are chewier and tastier than udon, and they are perhaps the favourite noodle of the Japanese. Udon and soba are not difficult to make at home, or they can be bought dried in the Japanese grocery stores now open in some of the larger cities in the West.

Udon (Wheat Flour Noodles)   *Serves 5–6*

4 oz (100 g) wholewheat flour   1 teaspoon salt
12 oz (350 g) plain white flour   about 5 fl oz (150 ml) water

Mix the flour and salt in a large bowl and then gradually add water to form a slightly dry dough. Knead for 10–15 minutes (a food processor or electric mixer may be used if available). Flour a board and roll out the dough into a thin (approximately ⅛ in/ 0.25 cm thick) rectangular sheet. Fold the 2 narrow ends of the sheet into the middle, and fold again at the middle to divide the dough into quarters. With a sharp knife cut the folded sheet crosswise into ⅛ in (0.25 cm) strips. Unroll the noodles and spread them on a floured board to await cooking. (For method see below.)

Soba (Buckwheat Flour Noodles)   *Serves 5–6*

1 lb (450 g) buckwheat flour   1 egg, beaten
1 teaspoon salt   about 4 fl oz (100 ml) water

Place the flour and salt in a large mixing bowl, thoroughly combine, add the beaten egg and stir in. Gradually add water to form a slightly dry dough. Knead for 10–15 minutes (a food processor or electric mixer may be used if available). Proceed as for udon noodles.

To cook udon and soba
Boil 4 pints (2.2 litres) water, carefully lower in the soba or udon, and return the water to the boil. Add 8 fl oz (225 ml) cold water and bring to the boil for a second time. Reduce the heat, and simmer until the noodles are cooked but still just hard at the core (approximately 10 minutes). This method of cooking ensures that both the inside and outside of the noodles are evenly cooked. Drain the noodles and rinse them under cold running water, separating any that are stuck together. To reheat, pour boiling water over the noodles.

Note The water in which the noodles were cooked may be reserved and used for preparing soup stock.

Udon or Soba in Soup Stock *Serves 4*

12 oz (350 g) fresh udon *or* soba, cooked and drained
2 pints (1.1 litres) vegetable soup stock, boiling
soya sauce to taste
garnish
one or more selected from:
    finely chopped chives
    finely chopped spring onions
    parboiled carrot slices
    slices of bamboo shoot *or* lotus root, heated through
    fresh or frozen garden peas, cooked
    slices of mushrooms sautéed in a little oil
    slices of hardboiled egg

Divide the cooked noodles among 4 bowls. Pour the boiling stock over them. Add soya sauce to taste, a selection of garnishes, and serve.

Chinese Vegetables in Sauce with Plain Soft Fried Noodles *Serves 6*

This dish can also be made with plain boiled noodles, if you prefer.

vegetables in sauce
- 2 Chinese dried mushrooms
- 4 tablespoons (60 ml) oil
- ½ teaspoon salt
- 1 sweet red *or* green pepper, seeded and cut into 1½ in (3 cm) wide diamond shapes
- 1 medium onion, halved and cut into ½ in (1 cm) wide strips
- 2 carrots, sliced diagonally into 2 in (5 cm) thick pieces
- 3 oz (75 g) bamboo shoots, thickly sliced
- 3 oz (75 g) water chestnuts, thickly sliced
- 2 oz (50 g) beansprouts
- 4 oz (100 g) fresh mushrooms, whole, or halved if large
- 4 tablespoons (60 ml) water
- 2 tablespoons (30 ml) soya sauce
- 1 tablespoon (15 ml) rice wine *or* medium sweet sherry
- ½ teaspoon sugar
- 1 tablespoon cornflour dissolved in 2 tablespoons (30 ml) water
- ½ teaspoon (2.5 ml) sesame oil

noodles
- 1 lb (450 g) egg noodles, cooked, rinsed under cold water and drained
- 4 tablespoons (60 ml) vegetable oil
- 6 spring onions, sliced
- ½ teaspoon salt
- 1 teaspoon (5 ml) soya sauce

To prepare the vegetables in sauce, first soak the dried mushrooms in hot water for 20 minutes. Drain, cut off the woody stems and slice the caps thickly. Heat 2 tablespoons (30 ml) oil in a large wok or frying pan. Add half the salt and stir fry for 30 seconds. Add the pepper and the onion and stir fry for 1 minute. Remove the vegetables from the pan. Add another 1 tablespoon (15 ml) oil. Put in the carrots and bamboo shoots and cook for 1½ minutes. Add the water chestnuts and fry for another minute. Sprinkle with the remainder of the salt, add the beansprouts, dried mushrooms, fresh mushrooms, water, soya sauce, sherry and sugar and bring quickly to the boil. Return all the vegetables to the pan and bring to the boil again. Then cover, reduce the heat a little and cook for 1½–2 minutes. Stir in the cornflour dissolved in water and sesame oil.

Mix the cooked noodles with 1 tablespoon (15 ml) vegetable oil. Heat the remaining oil in a pan until quite hot, add the spring onions and stir fry for 30 seconds. Add the noodles, salt and soya sauce and stir fry for another ½–1 minute or until completely heated through and lightly browned. Serve in a nice big bowl with the Chinese vegetables, which should be very hot.

Casserole Noodles with Floating Eggs   Serves 4

Japan

- 12 oz (350 g) noodles, cooked until not quite tender, drained and rinsed under cold water
- 2 pints (1.1 litres) vegetable stock *or* water
- 2 tablespoons (30 ml) soya sauce
- 3 tablespoons (45 ml) medium sweet sherry *or* mirin
- 2 teaspoons sugar
- 4 oz (100 g) button mushrooms, washed
- 2 small leeks, cut into 2 in (5 cm) lengths
- 4 medium eggs

garnish
- 2 tablespoons finely chopped parsley
- black pepper *or* togarashi to taste

Place the parboiled noodles in a large oven-to-table casserole dish and add the stock, soya sauce, sherry and sugar. Bring to a slow boil, lower in the mushrooms and leeks, and carefully break in the eggs so that they remain separate from one another. Cover the dish and gently simmer until the eggs are cooked. Take the casserole dish to the table, garnish with parsley and black pepper and serve.

Deep Fried Noodles (Yaki Soba)   Serves 4

Yaki soba was the first dish I learned to order in Japanese. The name rolls off the tongue and the pronunciation is easy, but that is not the only reason for asking for it. The Japanese are masters at deep frying, and yaki soba allows this talent full expression.

- 2 tablespoons (30 ml) vegetable oil
- 1 clove garlic, crushed
- 2 teaspoons finely grated root ginger
- 1 medium onion, quartered and each quarter halved
- 1 green pepper, seeded and cut into ½ in (1.25 cm) strips
- 4 oz (100 g) mushrooms, sliced
- 8 oz (225 g) noodles, cooked, drained, rinsed under cold water, drained again and rubbed with a little oil
- oil for deep frying
- 2 teaspoons cornflour blended with a little water
- 1 tablespoon (15 ml) soya sauce

Heat the oil in a saucepan and sauté the garlic and ginger for 1 minute. Add the onion and green pepper and sauté for another 2–3 minutes. Stir in the mushrooms and let them soften. Add to the pan enough water barely to cover the vegetables. Bring to the boil and then set to simmer.

Meanwhile deep fry the noodles. Heat 4 in (10 cm) oil in a deep frying pan to 350°F (175°C). Separate the noodles into strands and drop handfuls at a time into the hot oil. Fry until lightly browned. Remove them with a basket or chopsticks and set aside to drain. Repeat for all the noodles.

Add the cornflour and soya sauce to the simmering vegetables and cook until the mixture thickens. Divide the deep fried noodles among 4 bowls, pour the sauce over them and serve immediately.

Summer Noodles *Serves 4*

The Japanese enjoy cold many foods that we in the West expect to eat hot. Chilled noodles are a great favourite, particularly in the summer, when stallholders appear on the streets selling bowls of hiyashi somen. For a Western summer meal they would make a welcome change from our usual salads and sandwiches.

12 oz (350 g) noodles, cooked, drained and chilled
1½ pints (825 ml) soup stock, chilled
3 tablespoons (45 ml) medium sweet sherry *or* mirin
2 tablespoons (30 ml) soya sauce

pinch cayenne
garnish
2 teaspoons grated root ginger
3–4 tablespoons parsley *or* watercress *or* spring onions *or* young spinach leaves, finely chopped

Divide the soba among 4 bowls. Combine the stock, sherry, soya sauce and cayenne and divide among 4 more small bowls. Place the ginger and parsley etc. in central bowls and invite the guests to garnish their own noodles. Dip the noodles into the individual bowls of sauce and eat.

Japanese Egg Noodles with Side Salad *Serves 4*

Ramen, or Japanese egg noodles with vegetables in hot soup, is a popular small restaurant meal in Japan. It goes well with a simple, fresh, crunchy salad, and served in this way provides a meal that is filling, nutritious and quick.

- 1 tablespoon (15 ml) vegetable oil
- 2 cloves garlic, crushed
- 2 spring onions, chopped
- 4 oz (100 g) beansprouts
- 1½ pints (825 ml) vegetable soup stock
- 2 tablespoons (30 ml) soya sauce *or* use miso for a more strongly flavoured dish
- ¼ teaspoon cayenne *or* seven spices pepper

side salad
- 2 tablespoons (30 ml) rice vinegar *or* cider vinegar
- 1 tablespoon (15 ml) vegetable oil
- 1 tablespoon sesame seeds, dry roasted
- salt and black pepper to taste
- ½ cucumber, sliced
- 1 bunch radishes, washed

plus
- 8 oz (225 g) egg noodles, cooked and drained (reheated when required by pouring boiling water over them in a colander)

Sauté the garlic in the oil in a saucepan until lightly golden. Add the spring onions and beansprouts and sauté a further 2–3 minutes. Add the soup stock and soya sauce (if miso is used, cream it first with a little soup stock) and bring to the boil. Add the cayenne. Set to simmer and prepare the side salad. Combine the vinegar, oil and sesame seeds. Arrange the cucumber and radishes in an attractive pattern in a bowl and pour the dressing over them. Reheat the cooked noodles and divide them among 4 bowls. Pour the hot soup over them and serve with the side salad.

Egg Dishes

Eggs are appreciated in the Far East as much as in the West for their nutritiousness and versatility. Most peasant families in the East, as in many other parts of the world, keep their own chickens and they run free, picking up food wherever it can be gleamed. Eggs not needed by the household are sold in local city markets, and of course they taste much better than the anaemic battery chicken eggs that we need to avoid in our own shops. In Eastern countries eggs are cooked by boiling, frying and steaming, and sometimes served with sauces. The recipes I have given here have been chosen for their combination of simplicity and distinctive difference from conventional Western egg recipes.

Spinach Rolled Omelette

Eggs on a Vegetable Nest

Chinese Steamed Omelette

Hardboiled Eggs with Hot Sauce

Soya Eggs with Plum Sauce

Quick Fried Cabbage with Eggs

Japanese Pancakes
Chinese Eggs and Tomatoes
Chinese Tea Eggs
Foo Yong Eggs and Cashew Nuts

Spinach Rolled Omelette *Makes 1 rolled omelette to serve 2 people*

This is a Westernized version of the Japanese rolled omelette. The cooking method given here is simpler than the traditional version, and a circular frying pan is used rather than the traditional rectangular shape. Serve as a starter or as part of a main course. Alternatively serve as a main dish with a sauce.

4 eggs
1 teaspoon (5 ml) soya sauce
¼ teaspoon ground ginger
1 teaspoon sugar
1 tablespoon finely sifted plain flour
10 young spinach leaves, washed and drained
1 stick celery, cut into long thin strips
1 tablespoon (15 ml) vegetable oil

Beat together the eggs, soya sauce, ginger, sugar and flour to form a smooth batter. Heat a heavy 9 in (22.5 cm) frying pan over a moderate flame until hot, and then lightly brush it with oil. Pour in half the batter mixture and tilt the pan so that the mixture spreads evenly. Cook until the underside is just soft but not browned. Turn the omelette over and repeat for the other side. Transfer the omelette to a plate and, if necessary, keep warm in a preheated moderate oven. Repeat for the remaining batter.

Trim each omelette into an approximate rectangle and keep the trimmings. Place one omelette on top of the other on a bamboo mat or slightly damp cloth, and across one end layer the omelette trimmings, the spinach leaves and the celery strips. Roll the omelette up like a Swiss roll and then remove the bamboo mat or cloth. Cut the roll into 1 in (2.5 cm) thick slices and serve.

Eggs on a Vegetable Nest *Serves 4*

China
Delicious served with Chinese Pancakes (see Noodle Dishes chapter).

3 Chinese dried mushrooms *or* 4 oz (100 g) sliced fresh mushrooms
4 eggs
pinch salt
3 tablespoons (45 ml) oil
1 oz (25 g) bamboo shoots, finely chopped
2 oz (50 g) carrot, thinly sliced

4 oz (100 g) beansprouts, washed and drained
3 spring onions, cut into 1 in (2.5 cm) lengths
1 tablespoon (15 ml) soya sauce
3 tablespoons (45 ml) vegetable stock
1 teaspoon (5 ml) rice wine *or* medium sweet sherry

If using dried mushrooms, soak in hot water for 30 minutes. Squeeze dry, discard the woody stems and dice the caps. Beat the eggs with the salt. Heat 1 tablespoon (15 ml) oil in a frying pan and stir fry the mushrooms for 1 minute, then add the bamboo shoots, carrot, beansprouts, spring onions, soya sauce, stock and rice wine. Cook for a further 1 minute. Turn out onto a warmed plate and keep on one side.

Add 2 tablespoons (30 ml) more oil to the pan and reheat. Turn down the heat and pour in the eggs. Cook as you would an omelette. When the egg is set on the bottom but still runny on top, return the vegetables to the pan with a slotted spoon. Cook for a further 30 seconds, then turn out onto a heated serving plate.

Chinese Steamed Omelette   *Serves 4*

In this dish the egg yolks are separated from the whites, which are then whisked with the other ingredients. The egg white mixture is poured into a deep dish and the yolks are arranged individually on top. The omelette is then steamed. The way to do this is to stand the dish containing the omelette on top of a smaller upturned plate in a large saucepan or casserole. Add 1 in (2.5 cm) of water to the pan and steam the omelette.

4 eggs
2 oz (50 g) mushrooms, chopped
1 tablespoon finely chopped onion
1 tablespoon finely chopped water chestnuts

1 tablespoon (15 ml) soya sauce
1 teaspoon (5 ml) rice wine *or* medium sweet sherry
1 tablespoon (15 ml) water
½ teaspoon (2.5 ml) vegetable oil

Separate the yolks from the whites of the eggs and set them aside, keeping each yolk in a separate saucer. Put the egg whites in a mixing bowl and whisk them together. Add all the remaining ingredients except the oil, and mix well. Pour the mixture into a deep dish (about 9 in/22.5 cm in diameter) that has been brushed with oil. Arrange the whole yolks in a neat pattern on top of the whites mixture. Steam the omelette for 15 minutes or until set. Serve.

Hardboiled Eggs with Hot Sauce   *Serves 4–6*

Indonesia
Serve as a side dish, or with vegetables and rice as a light meal.

sauce
3 tablespoons (45 ml) vegetable oil
1 medium onion, finely sliced
½–1 teaspoon chilli powder *or* hot pepper sauce
8 oz (225 g) ripe tomatoes, peeled and chopped

1 teaspoon white sugar
salt to taste
juice of ½ lemon
plus
4–6 hardboiled eggs, shelled and halved

Heat the oil in a saucepan, add the onion and sauté it until lightly browned. Add the chilli powder, tomatoes and sugar and cook, stirring, until the tomatoes have pulped. Season with salt and lemon juice. Mix well and simmer the sauce, uncovered, for 5 minutes.

Put the eggs in the sauce and heat them thoroughly for 3–4 minutes, spooning the sauce over the eggs. Alternatively, leave the eggs to marinate in the sauce for 1–2 hours, reheat and serve.

Soya Eggs with Plum Sauce   *Serves 4*

China
Serve as a hot accompaniment to a meal or cold as an appetizer. Plum sauce is thick, like chutney, it is available in tins from Chinese grocery stores.

4 eggs
8 fl oz (225 ml) soya sauce
8 fl oz (225 ml) vegetable stock
6 tablespoons sugar
few drops sesame oil

1 tablespoon grated onion
16–20 radishes, washed and trimmed
plum sauce

Place the eggs in a saucepan, cover them with cold water, bring to the boil and boil gently for 5 minutes. Remove from the heat and run the eggs under cold water for another 5 minutes. Remove their shells carefully. Put the soya sauce, stock, sugar, sesame oil and onions in a small saucepan. Bring the mixture to boiling point. Add the eggs, cover the pan and simmer for 10 minutes. Remove the pan from the heat and allow the eggs to cool in the sauce for 30 minutes. (Turn the eggs during the cooking and cooling to ensure that they are covered evenly.) Drain the eggs and cut into quarters lengthwise. Serve with radishes and plum sauce.

Quick Fried Cabbage with Eggs   *Serves 2–4*

Indonesia

1 tablespoon (15 ml) vegetable oil
1 medium onion, finely sliced
8 oz (225 g) cabbage *or* Chinese cabbage, finely shredded
salt and pepper to taste
pinch chilli powder
2 eggs, beaten

Heat the oil in a heavy frying pan or wok and fry the onion in it until softened. Add the cabbage, salt, pepper and chilli powder. Stir fry for 2–3 minutes and then cover the pan and cook the mixture over a low heat for 10 minutes. Now stir in the beaten eggs and scramble them with the cabbage. As soon as the eggs have set, serve.

Japanese Pancakes   *Serves 2–3*

One of my most enjoyable restaurant meals in Japan was in a 'cook it yourself' pancake house in Tokyo. The restaurant was on the eighth floor of a ten-storey building, and on every level there were numerous other restaurants, each specializing in a particular type of cooking. The pancake place was lined with low tables, each inset with a big hotplate. Each diner was given a large bowl containing a bottom layer of vegetables and fish (not included in the recipe given here) and topped with a raw egg.

We seasoned our bowls of food with a variety of sauces, mixed it all together and then proceeded to fry portions on the hot plate. We cooked delicious pancakes, each custom-made. Finally, as a last course, we were served a huge tray of cooked noodles and fresh vegetables to fry.

You may wish to prepare these pancakes in the manner described above, using an electric frying pan at the table, but otherwise cook them in the kitchen and keep them warm in a preheated moderate oven until you are ready to serve.

3 oz (75 g) plain flour
3 fl oz (75 ml) water
3 medium eggs
1 teaspoon (5 ml) soya sauce
½ medium onion, diced
4 oz (100 g) mushrooms, thinly sliced
1 medium red *or* green pepper, seeded and chopped
2 oz (50 g) French beans, cut into 2 in (5 cm) lengths, parboiled for 2 minutes, drained and rinsed in cold water
2 tablespoons (30 ml) vegetable oil

Put the flour, water and eggs into a mixing bowl and beat into a smooth batter. Add the soya sauce, onion, mushrooms, pepper and French beans. Mix well. Heat half the oil in a heavy 9 in (22.5 cm) frying pan and pour in half the mixture. Cook over a low heat until the bottom side is set and lightly browned. Turn the pancake over and brown the other side. Transfer to the oven to keep warm and repeat for the remaining batter and oil.

Chinese Eggs and Tomatoes   *Serves 4*

6 eggs
1½ tablespoons (25 ml) rice wine *or* medium sweet sherry
pinch salt
2 tablespoons (30 ml) vegetable oil
1¼ lb (550 g) tomatoes, skinned and thickly sliced
4 tablespoons (60 ml) vegetable stock
garnish
2 spring onions, finely chopped

Beat the eggs with the rice wine and salt. Heat the oil in a frying pan and fry the tomato slices over a moderate heat. Add a little salt and then the beaten egg mixture. Stir fry for 1 minute, as for scrambled eggs. Pour in the stock and cook for a further minute. Serve immediately, very hot, sprinkled with the chopped spring onions.

Chinese Tea Eggs

Serves 5

The eggs may be prepared in advance but do not shell them until ready to serve. Serve halved or quartered as an appetizer, or as a garnish for a luncheon salad.

4 eggs
1¼ pints (750 ml) boiling water
2 tablespoons Indian tealeaves
1 teaspoon salt
2 cloves star anise

Put the eggs in a saucepan and cover them with cold water. Bring to the boil over a high heat. Reduce the heat and simmer for 5 minutes. Remove the eggs from the heat, drain and run cold water over them for 5 minutes. Dry the eggs and tap the shells gently on all sides to crack them evenly. Place the boiling water in a saucepan with the tea, salt and star anise. Add the eggs, cover, and simmer gently for 1½ hours. Let the eggs cool in the flavoured water for 30 minutes.

Foo Yong Eggs and Cashew Nuts

Serves 4–6

China

3 Chinese dried mushrooms *or* 4 oz (100 g) sliced fresh mushrooms
2 tablespoons (30 ml) vegetable oil
3 spring onions, finely chopped
1 clove garlic, crushed
1 piece root ginger about 1 in (2.5 cm) long, finely chopped
1 oz (25 g) canned bamboo shoots, diced
6 canned water chestnuts, chopped
6 oz (175 g) cashew nuts
1 tablespoon (15 ml) dry sherry
salt
6 eggs, beaten

If using dried mushrooms, soak them in warm water for 30 minutes. Squeeze them dry, discard the woody stalks, and chop the caps. Heat the oil in a deep frying pan, add the spring onions, garlic and ginger and stir fry for 1 minute. Add the mushrooms, bamboo shoots and water chestnuts and cook for a further 30 seconds. Stir in the nuts and sherry and season with salt. Lower the heat and pour in the beaten eggs. Scramble until the mixture is just set. Pile onto a warmed serving dish, garnish with chopped spring onions and serve.

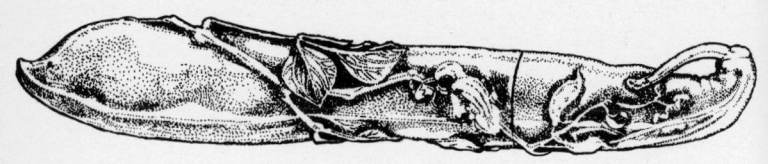

Beancurd (Tofu) and Tempe Dishes

Beancurd, or tofu in Japanese, is a fermented soya bean product introduced into the Far East by the Chinese. It is cheap to produce and provides a valuable source of protein and minerals. It can be used in some of the ways in which we use cheese in Western cookery. Unlike cheese, however, tofu contains no fat, and has the property of aiding the digestion of other foods. Tofu is white and has the consistency of light custard. It is usually bought in squares about 3 × 3 in (7.5 × 7.5 cm) and 1 in (2.5 cm) deep. Cut into cubes and added to soups, vegetables or salad dishes, it is delicious. Fried beancurd has a yellow, firm crust and is generally used in cooked dishes in which fresh beancurd would break up. Stored under water, tofu will keep for 2–3 days in the refrigerator.

Shops where tofu is made and sold are common all over Japan. The tofu man is a common sight walking through the streets with his hand-cart and trays of freshly made tofu. Like many other Japanese pursuits, making tofu has acquired the status of an art, but it can be made at home in the traditional manner. The process is quite long-winded; see *The Book of Tofu*, by N. Shurtlerf and A. Aoyagi (Autumn Press, Mass. 1975), for further information. In this book I give a quick recipe for making tofu, using only soya flour and lemon juice, but for most practical purposes it is much easier to buy ready-made tofu from health food stores or Chinese grocery shops.

Tempe is made by combining soaked soya beans with an enzyme-producing agent such as yeast which breaks down the beans and then binds them together. This makes the beans easier to digest. Tempe is sold in slabs in which the individual beans can be seen. The surface of the slabs develops a white skin similar to that found on some cheeses, e.g. Brie. The texture of tempe ranges from soft to crunchy and the taste is slightly nutty. Tempe is an excellent source of protein, vitamin, carbohydrates and minerals and it is an important nutritional food in South East Asia. Tempe is just becoming available in the better stocked wholefood shops. It's worth trying if you can find a stockist.

Home-made Beancurd

Fried Beancurd and Dipping Sauce

Sweet and Sour Vegetable and Beancurd Salad

Beancurd with Broad Beans

Mixed Vegetables and Beancurd

Beancurd and Vegetable Curry

Fried Tempe

Seasoned and Fried Tempe

Fried Tempe in Hot Sauce

Home-made Beancurd

1 lb (450 g) soya beans	3 tablespoons (45 ml) fresh lemon juice

Cover the soya beans with water and leave to soak for at least 12 hours. Change the water once during soaking. Drain, and grind the beans in either an electric grinder or a hand mill. Transfer to a heavy pot and add 2½ times as much water by volume as beans. Bring to the boil, reduce heat and simmer for 1 hour. Arrange 3–4 layers of cheesecloth inside a colander placed over a large pan. Strain the contents of the pan through this. Finally, gather the cheesecloth around the collected pulp and squeeze out as much as possible of the remaining liquid into the pan. Transfer the collected liquid to a glass bowl. Add lemon juice to it, stir once, cover with a damp cloth and leave in a warm spot (80°F, 120°C is perfect) for 8–12 hours or until the beancurd sets. Drain through cheesecloth to remove excess liquid. The beancurd may now be used. For a professional look, pour it into a square mould, put a light weight on top and press for 4 hours. Store under water in a refrigerator.

For flavoured beancurd, simmer a block or small squares in oil and soya sauce with mint, garlic, nutmeg, cinnamon, cloves, fennel, black pepper or whatever seasoning you like.

Fried Beancurd and Dipping Sauce

China
Roll pieces of beancurd about 3 in (6 cm) square in cornflour, taking care not to break them. Then deep fry them over a moderate heat for 4 minutes until light golden in colour. Lift the beancurd out carefully and drain. Eat hot with one of the following sauces, made simply by combining the ingredients listed.

Dipping Sauce 1
¼ teaspoon (2.5 ml) chilli oil
1 clove garlic, crushed
2 teaspoons grated root ginger
2 spring onions, finely chopped

Dipping Sauce 2
2 tablespoons (30 ml) medium sweet sherry *or* rice wine
3 tablespoons (45 ml) dark soya sauce
1 teaspoon sugar

Dipping Sauce 3
3 tablespoons (45 ml) dark soya sauce
1 tablespoon prepared mustard
1 teaspoon dark brown sugar
1 teaspoon (5 ml) rice vinegar *or* cider vinegar
1 teaspoon minced spring onion

Sweet and Sour Vegetable and Beancurd Salad Serves 4–6

Cubes of beancurd are marinated in a sweet and sour dressing and then mixed with raw chopped vegetables and mushrooms in this Western adaptation of a South East Asian salad.

2 tablespoons (30 ml) sesame oil
3 tablespoons (45 ml) soya sauce
3 tablespoons (45 ml) cider vinegar
1 tablespoon (15 ml) water
1 teaspoon (5 ml) clear honey
1 clove garlic, crushed

2 blocks (total weight 12 oz/ 300 g) beancurd, cut into 1 in (2.5 cm) cubes
2 stalks celery, finely chopped
2 oz (50 g) mushrooms, washed and sliced
4 oz (100 g) Chinese or white cabbage, finely shredded

Combine the oil, soya sauce, vinegar, water, honey and garlic and mix well together. Put two-thirds of this mixture into a large shallow bowl or container and add the beancurd cubes. Leave them to marinate in the refrigerator for 1 hour.

Transfer the beancurd and marinade to a serving bowl and gently stir in the celery, mushrooms and cabbage. Add the remaining dressing, carefully toss the salad and serve.

Beancurd with Broad Beans Serves 4

China

3 tablespoons (45 ml) peanut oil
6 oz (175 g) small broad beans
12 oz (350 g) beancurd, cut into 1 in (2.5 cm) cubes
1 oz (25 g) Szechwan preserved vegetables, finely chopped (optional; see pp. 19 and 65)
1 tablespoon (15 ml) light soya sauce

½ pint (275 ml) vegetable stock
8 oz (225 g) button mushrooms, wiped and the stalk ends trimmed
thickening
2 teaspoons cornflour
4 teaspoons (20 ml) water
garnish
1 teaspoon (5 ml) sesame oil

Heat a wok or frying pan with the oil and stir fry the beans with a little salt for about 1½ minutes. Add the beancurd cubes and continue cooking for another 30 seconds over a moderate heat. Then add the preserved vegetables (if used), soya sauce and stock. Bring to the boil. Add the mushrooms and simmer gently for

5 minutes. Adjust the seasoning if necessary. Combine the thickening ingredients and stir into the vegetables until the sauce thickens. Serve very hot, sprinkled with the sesame seed oil.

Mixed Vegetables and Beancurd   Serves 6–8

Japanese
Beancurd is an excellent ingredient in mixed vegetable dishes – it absorbs the flavours of other ingredients and links them together. The vegetables given in the recipe are only suggestions, and you should choose from whatever is available.

2 tablespoons (30 ml) vegetable oil
1 clove garlic, crushed
1 medium onion, thinly sliced
4 oz (100 g) cabbage, coarsely chopped
4 oz (100 g) broccoli, cut into florets *and/or* 4 oz (100 g) sprouts, quartered
1 small aubergine, sliced, salted, rinsed and drained
2 stalks celery, cut into ½ in (1.25 cm) lengths
4 oz (100 g) French beans, cut into 1 in (2.5 cm) lengths
1 medium green pepper, peeled and cut into 1 in (2.5 cm) strips

1 bamboo shoot, sliced into half moons (optional)
2 oz (50 g) mushrooms, sliced
1 teaspoon salt
1 teaspoon black pepper
2 tablespoons (30 ml) soya sauce
10 fl oz (300 ml) soup stock *or* water
6 oz (175 g) beancurd cut into 1 in (2.5 cm) cubes and deep fried (see p. 136)
2 tablespoons (30 ml) mirin *or* medium sweet sherry (optional)

Heat the oil in an oven-to-table casserole, add the garlic and sauté for 1 minute, add the onions and lightly brown. Add all the remaining vegetables and stir fry for 3–4 minutes. Add all the remaining ingredients except the beancurd and mirin, bring to the boil, reduce the heat and simmer for 10 minutes. Drop in the beancurd and simmer for a further 10 minutes. Finally pour in the mirin, and serve the dish from the casserole.

Beancurd and Vegetable Curry   Serves 4

Thailand
Almost any type of vegetables may be used in this curry. The

method is simple and does not, as in most Thai curries, use coconut milk.

2 tablespoons (30 ml) vegetable oil	1 lb (450 g) vegetables, e.g.: cauliflower, cut into florets
2 cloves garlic, crushed	Chinese cabbage, coarsely shredded
½ medium onion, finely chopped	fresh mushrooms, sliced
12 oz (350 g) pressed beancurd cut into 1 in (2.5 cm) cubes	green beans, cut into 2 in (5 cm) lengths
½ pint (275 ml) water *or* stock	tinned bamboo shoots, sliced
1–2 tablespoons mild curry powder	*garnish*
2 tablespoons (30 ml) lemon juice	coriander leaves, finely chopped
2 tablespoons (30 ml) soya sauce	

Heat the oil in a saucepan or wok and sauté the garlic and onion until golden. Add the beancurd and water and bring to the boil. Reduce the heat and simmer, uncovered, for 2–3 minutes. With a slotted spoon, lift out about one-third of the beancurd cubes and transfer them to the goblet of a blender. Add 4 fl oz (100 ml) of liquid from the pan, together with the curry powder, lemon juice and soya sauce. Blend the mixture smooth and return it to the pan. Add the vegetables to the pan, leaving until last those with the shortest cooking time, and simmer, uncovered, until tender (about 10 minutes). Garnish with coriander leaves and serve.

Fried Tempe   *Serves 4*

Indonesia

Fried tempe is delicious served as a snack or side dish lightly sprinkled with salt or accompanied by a sambal dipping sauce. It is also the basic ingredient of the two tempe recipes that follow this one.

12 oz (350 g) tempe, cut into sticks about 2 × ¼ × ½ in (5 × 1 × ½ cm)	oil for deep frying salt to taste

Heat about 1 in (2.5 cm) of oil in a deep frying pan over a medium flame. Add half the tempe sticks and fry, stirring, until they turn golden brown (about 5 minutes). Remove them with a small sieve or slotted spoon and set them to drain on absorbent kitchen paper. Repeat for the remaining tempe. Combine the 2 batches of tempe, sprinkle with salt and serve.

Seasoned and Fried Tempe   *Serves 4*

Indonesia

ingredients for fried tempe recipe
plus
2 cloves garlic, crushed
1 teaspoon salt
½ teaspoon freshly ground pepper
1 teaspoon ground coriander
4 fl oz (100 ml) water
juice of 1 lemon *or* 3 tablespoons (45 ml) tamarind water

Mix all the ingredients together in a bowl and add half the tempe sticks. Stir them about in the bowl to coat each stick with the seasoning. Leave them to marinate for 5–10 minutes. Place a sieve over a bowl. Remove the sticks and leave them to drain for a few minutes in the sieve. Deep fry the seasoned tempe as described in the fried tempe recipe. Repeat for the remaining tempe.

Fried Tempe in Hot Sauce   *Serves 4*

Indonesia

ingredients for fried tempe recipe
plus
1 medium onion, finely chopped
2 cloves garlic
2 fresh *or* dried red chillies, seeded
2 fl oz (50 ml) water
2 teaspoons brown sugar
1 teaspoon salt

Fry the tempe sticks as described in the fried tempe recipe and keep them warm in a hot oven. Put the onion, garlic, chillies and water into a blender or food processor and blend them to a paste. Remove all but 2 tablespoons (30 ml) of oil from the frying pan in which the tempe was fried. Add the paste and stir fry for 4–5 minutes. Stir in the sugar and salt, and then the fried tempe. Mix well and serve immediately.

Desserts

Throughout the Far East a meal is more likely to be finished with a basket of fruit than with a sweet dessert. There are no set customs that a meal should be ended with something sweet, and desserts as we know them are more popular as between-meal snacks, or else they are reserved for banquets and formal dinners. Having said that, there are of course many delicious sweet dishes in the East, often available ready-made in markets or prepared on the spot by roadside vendors. I have selected for this chapter a number that are both easy to prepare in a Western kitchen and contain readily available ingredients. Several of the recipes use bananas and/or coconut, and this reflects the popularity and accessibility of these two foods in all the South East Asian countries.

Fruit Tempura with Honey

Toffee Fruit

Chinese Almond Biscuits

Banana Pancakes

Coconut Filled Pancakes

Coconut Batter Pancakes

Sticky Rice with Mangoes

Baked Ginger and Citrus Bananas

Shallow Fried Bananas

Deep Fried Bananas

Fried Ball Cake

Baked Coconut Custard

Crackling Bananas (and Pears and Apples)

Almond Custard in Orange-flower Syrup

Festive Rice Pudding

Fruit Tempura with Honey *Serves 4*

This is a similar method to the one used for the preparation of vegetable tempura, but the batter is thicker. The deep fried, batter-coated fruit is served in honey. For a toffee sauce variation, see below.

4 oz (100 g) plain flour
1 egg, lightly beaten
8 fl oz (225 ml) water

2 firm eating apples *or* pears *or* bananas, peeled and cut into mouth-size pieces
oil for deep frying
honey

Combine the flour, egg and water in a mixing bowl and beat it into a smooth batter. Pour into a deep frying pan oil to a depth of 2–3 in (5–7.5 cm). Heat the oil to 320–350°F (150–180°C) and keep it at this temperature. At 350°F (180°C) a small lump of batter dropped into the oil will cook golden brown in 1 minute. Using a pair of chopsticks, pick up one piece of fruit, dip it into the batter, shake off the excess and drop the coated fruit into the oil. Repeat for several pieces of fruit, but do not fry too much at once. Turn the fruit once during cooking if it looks necessary. Allow it to crisp and brown. Remove from the oil, shake off excess fat, and set the fruit to drain on absorbent paper. Once the first batch is cooked, remove any floating pieces of batter from the oil and then fry another portion. Be sure to keep the oil at the right temperature – if it gets too low, the fruit starts to absorb oil and you will get soggy tempura.

Divide the fruit tempura among 4 bowls, pour the honey over them and serve.

Toffee Fruit   *Serves 4*

Prepare Fruit Tempura as above but serve it in the following toffee sauce. Provide at the table a bowl of iced water to dip the toffee fruit into before eating.

8 oz (225 g) granulated sugar
4 fl oz (100 ml) water

1 tablespoon (15 ml) vegetable oil
1 tablespoon sesame seeds

Put the sugar, water and oil into a small, heavy-bottomed saucepan and bring the mixture to the boil, stirring. Boil and stir over a medium heat until the solution thickens and browns. Add the sesame seeds and remove from the heat. It is now ready.

Chinese Almond Biscuits   *Makes about 30 biscuits*

6 oz (175 g) butter
4 oz (100 g) caster sugar
½ teaspoon (2.5 ml) almond essence
7 oz (200 g) plain flour

about 30 blanched whole *or* split almonds
1 egg yolk
2 tablespoons (30 ml) water

Preheat the oven to 275°F (140°C, gas mark 1). Cream the butter with the sugar until light and fluffy and then stir in the almond essence. Mix in the flour, half at a time, with your fingers. The dough should be just crumbly. Form tablespoons of the dough into flat, round biscuits about 2 in (5 cm) in diameter by rolling the dough between your fingers into a ball shape and then flattening it out. Lightly grease a baking sheet and place the biscuits on it, close but not touching. Decorate the top of each with a single almond. Whisk the egg yolk and water together and brush the biscuits with the mixture. Bake for 30 minutes, then raise the oven temperature to 350°F (180°C, gas mark 4) and bake for a further 10 minutes. Allow the biscuits to cool a little on the baking sheet and then transfer to a wire rack to cool completely. Store them in an airtight tin or jar.

Banana Pancakes — *Serves 4*

Indonesia

2 eggs, beaten
½ teaspoon salt
4 oz (100 g) plain flour
½ pint (275 ml) milk (*or* fresh *or* canned coconut milk)
1 tablespoon white sugar

2 medium bananas, peeled and mashed
vegetable oil *or* butter for frying
lemon juice to taste

Beat the eggs and salt together in a mixing bowl. Whisk in the flour and then the milk to form a smooth batter. Stir in the sugar and bananas and beat the mixture well to eliminate any large lumps of banana. Alternatively, the ingredients for the batter could be put beaten until smooth in a food blender or processor.

Brush a heavy pan with oil and heat it over a moderate flame. Pour some batter into the pan and swirl it around to form a thin ¼ in (½ cm) coating on the surface. Lightly brown the bottom side of the pancake, then turn it over and brown the other side. Repeat for the remaining batter. Pile the cooked pancakes one on top of the other on a buttered plate and serve them sprinkled with lemon juice.

Coconut Filled Pancakes — *Serves 4*

Indonesia

batter
2 eggs, beaten
½ teaspoon salt
4 oz (100 g) plain flour
½ pint (275 ml) milk (*or* fresh *or* canned coconut milk)
vegetable oil *or* butter for frying

filling
4 oz (100 g) brown sugar
8 fl oz (225 ml) water
6 oz (175 g) desiccated coconut *or* grated fresh coconut
½ teaspoon (2.5 ml) vanilla essence (optional)
juice of ½ lemon

Beat the eggs and salt together in a mixing bowl. Whisk in the flour and then the milk, and beat the mixture to form a smooth batter. Set it aside, covered.

To make the filling, heat the sugar and water in a pan, stirring until the sugar is dissolved. Add the coconut and vanilla essence, if used, and simmer, stirring, until all the liquid has been absorbed by the coconut. Stir in the lemon juice and set the mixture aside.

Brush a heavy frying pan with oil and heat it over a moderate flame. Pour some batter into the pan and swirl it around to form a thin coating over the surface. Lightly brown the bottom side of the pancake and then turn it over and brown the other side. Repeat for the remaining batter. Pile the cooked pancakes one on top of the other on a buttered plate. Put some filling in each, roll it up and serve hot or cold.

Coconut Batter Pancakes   *Makes 12 pancakes*

The batter in this Thai recipe uses coconut milk instead of cow's milk. The coconut flavoured result makes an interesting change from ordinary pancakes.

1 pint (550 ml) thin coconut milk *or* 4 oz (100 g) creamed coconut blended with ¾ pint (450 ml) water
3 eggs, beaten
5 oz (150 g) rice flour *or* plain white flour
4 oz (100 g) desiccated coconut
3 oz white sugar
pinch salt
oil for frying
lemon juice

Preheat the oven to 325°F (170°C, gas mark 3). Combine all the ingredients and beat into a smooth batter. Wipe a 6–7 in (15–18 cm) frying pan with a little oil and place over a moderate heat. When hot, spoon in just enough batter to cover the bottom of the pan. Lightly brown one side of the pancake, then turn it over and repeat on the other side. Roll up the pancake and place on a warm plate in the oven. Repeat for all the batter. Serve sprinkled with lemon juice.

Sticky Rice with Mangoes   *Serves 4–6*

This Thai dessert is everyone's favourite during the mango season. If glutinous rice is unavailable, short grain pudding rice may be substituted.

½ pint (300 g) medium coconut milk
2 oz (50 g) white sugar
½ teaspoon salt
10 oz (300 g) glutinous (sticky) rice, soaked overnight, drained and cooked (it should be still warm)
4 ripe mangoes, peeled, halved, stoned and sliced crosswise

In a large mixing bowl stir 8 fl oz (225 ml) of the coconut milk together with the sugar and salt until the sugar dissolves. Stir in the still warm cooked rice, cover, and set aside for 20–30 minutes. Meanwhile, simmer the remaining coconut milk in a small pan, uncovered, for 10 minutes. Place the sticky rice in the centre of a serving plate, arrange the mango slices around it, sprinkle the rice with the simmered coconut milk and serve.

Baked Ginger and Citrus Bananas   *Serves 6*

This South East Asian dessert is particularly good and lends itself well to Western tastes and the Western kitchen.

2 oz (50 g) butter	½ teaspoon ground cinnamon
2 oz (50 g) white sugar	1 teaspoon grated lemon rind
1 tablespoon (15 ml) lemon juice	2 teaspoons finely chopped root ginger
1 tablespoon (15 ml) orange juice	6 bananas, peeled and cut in half crosswise

Preheat the oven to 375°F (190°C, gas mark 5). Beat together the butter and sugar, then beat in all the remaining ingredients except the bananas. Lightly grease a shallow baking dish and arrange the banana pieces on the bottom. Pour the mixture over them and bake for 15 minutes. Serve immediately.

Shallow Fried Bananas   *Serves 4*

Bananas of many varieties are abundant in Thailand. They are popular shallow fried and deep fried, both as street snacks and as desserts at home.

2 tablespoons (30 ml) peanut oil *or* butter	3 tablespoons brown *or* white sugar (according to taste)
4 firm bananas, peeled, sliced lengthwise and then crosswise to give 4 pieces per banana	lemon *or* lime juice to taste

Heat the oil in a wok or frying pan. Add the banana pieces and fry them on both sides over a moderate heat until very lightly browned. Spoon the sugar over them and gently stir it in until it dissolves. Transfer the bananas and sugar syrup to serving dishes, sprinkle with lemon juice and serve.

Desserts 147

Deep Fried Bananas
Serves 4

¼ pint (125 ml) water
5 oz (150 g) rice flour *or* plain white flour
1 egg, beaten
2 tablespoons desiccated coconut
pinch salt
4 firm bananas, peeled, sliced lengthwise and then crosswise to give 4 pieces per banana
oil for deep frying

Combine the water, flour, egg, coconut and salt in a mixing bowl and whisk into a smooth batter. Heat the oil for deep frying until it just starts to smoke. Dip the banana slices in the batter and fry them 5 or 6 at a time until golden brown and crisp. Remove them with a slotted spoon and drain on a paper towel before serving. Repeat for all the banana pieces.

Fried Ball Cake
Serves 6

Small balls of cake mixture are fried and served hot. This recipe is from Okinawa, Japan, where the cakes are traditionally made for engagement parties.

8 oz (225 g) plain flour
1 teaspoon baking powder
6 oz (175 g) caster sugar
2 eggs, lightly beaten
3 oz (75 g) peanuts, coarsely crushed
3 tablespoons (45 ml) vegetable oil

Sift the flour and baking powder into a mixing bowl. Add the sugar, eggs, peanuts and 1 tablespoon (15 ml) of the oil and beat the mixture together, by hand or in a food processor, to form a smooth dough. Cover the dough with a damp cloth and set aside in a cool place for 30 minutes. Form the dough into 1 in (2.5 cm) diameter balls and fry them in the remaining oil until lightly browned all over. Drain and serve hot.

Baked Coconut Custard
Serves 4–6

8 fl oz (225 ml) medium coconut milk
4 eggs, beaten
4 oz (100 g) light brown sugar
pinch salt

Preheat the oven to 350°F (180°C, gas mark 4). Whisk together all the ingredients in a saucepan over a moderate heat and cook, stirring continuously, until the mixture starts to thicken (about 7–8 minutes). Lightly grease a 9 in (22.5 cm) diameter flan or pie dish and pour in the mixture. Bake for 30 minutes or until the top is lightly browned. Allow to cool before cutting into portions.

Variation
In Thailand the coconut custard is prepared steamed inside a hollowed out coconut shell. Instead of pouring the custard mixture into a pie dish, pour it into a coconut shell with the top cut off and meat scraped out. Place the coconut on a plate on an upturned bowl in a pan with 1 in (2.5 cm) water in it, and steam for 30–40 minutes or until the custard is set. Chill and serve.

Crackling Bananas

China

8 fl oz (225 ml) honey
4 oz (100 g) sugar
4 fl oz (100 ml) water
1 teaspoon (5 ml) cider vinegar

1–2 barely ripe bananas per person
large shallow bowl of water with ice cubes in it

Put the honey, sugar, water and vinegar into a saucepan and cook until it reaches 275°F (140°C) (soft crack stage) on a sugar thermometer. Meanwhile, cut the bananas into 1 in (2 cm) chunks and arrange them in a shallow bowl. Have chopsticks handy; they are really the best implements for dealing with this dish. Prepare the iced water. When the syrup is ready, pour it over the banana chunks. Try to coat them thoroughly, but still handle the fruit gently. Take to the table quickly and serve. Each guest takes a piece of banana with his/her chopsticks and dips it in the iced water.

Variations
Crackling Pears
Make the syrup as above. Choose ripe but firm pears, one per person. Peel, core and cut each into 8 chunks. Sprinkle about ½ teaspoon freshly grated root ginger over the pears before pouring the syrup on top.

Crackling Apples
Make the syrup as before but omit the vinegar. Choose firm

fleshed apples such as Granny Smiths or Cox's Orange Pippins, one per person. Peel and core the apples and cut into 6 or 8 chunks each. Sprinkle with lemon juice to prevent discoloration while the syrup is cooking.

Almond Custard in Orange-flower Syrup

China

custard
2 pints (1.1 litres) milk
4 oz (100 g) ground almonds
sugar to taste
1 envelope unflavoured
 gelatine

orange-flavour syrup
2 tablespoons (30 ml) cold
 water
3 fl oz (75 ml) orange-flower
 water
2 tablespoons sugar

To make the orange-flower syrup, combine the water, sugar and half the orange-flower water. Stir until the sugar is dissolved. Boil for 5 minutes. Cool and add the remaining orange-flower water. Set aside in the refrigerator.

Heat the milk and ground almonds together just to simmering. Do not let the milk boil. Keep warm but not boiling for 20 minutes. Strain the mixture through 2 thicknesses of cheesecloth or muslin (wring out what is left to extract all the flavour from the almonds). Sweeten sparingly to taste. Soften the gelatine in a little cold water, then add it to the milk and almond mixture. Heat the mixture until the gelatine is dissolved, but do not let it boil. Pour the custard into individual serving dishes and put them in the refrigerator to chill and set. The mixture will not be very firm, just thickened. Serve very cold with the orange-flower syrup.

Festive Rice Pudding   *Serves 4–6*

This is a Westernized version of the famous Chinese dish called Light-Jewel Pudding.

8 oz (225 g) cooked rice
4 eggs
¾ pint (450 ml) milk

3 oz (75 g) candied fruits
1 teaspoon (5 ml) vanilla
 essence

Preheat the oven to 325°F (170°C, gas mark 3). Combine all the ingredients in a mixing bowl and pour the mixture into a greased soufflé dish. Set the dish in a larger pan of hot water. Bake for about 30 minutes. Test with a knife blade (if on withdrawing the blade it is clean, the pudding is cooked). Let the pudding stand for a few minutes before serving. If you can, make the pudding a few hours before needed; it is at its very best when just at room temperature.

Conversion Tables

Conversion of imperial measurements to metric:

Weights		Liquids	
Imperial	Approx. metric equivalent	Imperial	Approx. metric equivalent
½ oz	15 g	¼ teaspoon	1.25 ml
1 oz	25 g	½ teaspoon	2.5 ml
2 oz	50 g	1 teaspoon	5 ml
3 oz	75 g	2 teaspoons	10 ml
4 oz	100 g	1 tablespoon	15 ml
5 oz	150 g	2 tablespoons	30 ml
6 oz	175 g	3 tablespoons	45 ml
7 oz	200 g	1 fl oz	25 ml
8 oz	225 g	2 fl oz	50 ml
9 oz	250 g	3 fl oz	75 ml
10 oz	275 g	4 fl oz	100 ml
11 oz	300 g	5 fl oz (¼ pint)	150 ml
12 oz	350 g	6 fl oz	175 ml
13 oz	375 g	7 fl oz	200 ml
14 oz	400 g	8 fl oz	225 ml
15 oz	425 g	9 fl oz	250 ml
1 lb	450 g	10 fl oz (½ pint)	275 ml
2 lb	900 g	15 fl oz (¾ pint)	450 ml
3 lb	1.4 kg	20 fl oz (1 pint)	550 ml
		1¾ pints	1 litre
		2 pints	1.1 litres

Exact conversion:
1 oz = 28.35 g

Oven temperatures

F°	C°	Gas Mark
225	110	¼
250	130	½
275	140	1
300	150	2
325	170	3
350	180	4
375	190	5
400	200	6
425	220	7
450	230	8
475	240	9

Index

aduki beans: red rice, 95–6
almonds: almond custard in orange-flower syrup, 149
Chinese almond biscuits, 143
apples: apples and grapes with Japanese mustard dressing, 76
carrot and apple salad, 71–2
crackling apples, 148–9
green apples with sweet hot sauce, 39
aubergines: aubergines and tomatoes cooked with soya sauce, 81–2
braised aubergines with peppers and onions, 89–90
fried aubergine salad, 73
fried aubergines, 82
spicy aubergines, 81

bamboo shoots, 30
bamboo shoot and green bean soup, 53–4
bananas: baked ginger and citrus bananas, 146
banana pancakes, 144
crackling bananas, 148
deep fried bananas, 147
shallow fried bananas, 146
bao (steamed filled buns), 45–6
bean paste, 18
beancurd (tofu), 17–18, 134–9
beancurd and broccoli fried rice, 103–4
beancurd and vegetable curry, 138–9
beancurd dressing, 77
beancurd with broad beans, 137–8

clear soup with lemon and beancurd, 58
fried beancurd and dipping sauce, 136
home-made, 135–6
Japanese white dressing, 77–8
lemon, beancurd and coconut milk soup, 52
mixed vegetables and beancurd, 138
oden, 86
sweet and sour vegetable and beancurd salad, 137
Thai curried beancurd with vegetables, 90
beansprouts, 30
beansprout and cucumber salad, 74
Chinese egg rolls, 40–1
mixed-up beansprout salad, 74
rice and beansprouts, 100
biscuits, Chinese almond, 143
black bean bao, 45–6
broadbeans, beancurd with, 137–8
broccoli: beancurd and broccoli fried rice, 103–4
broccoli with lemon and coconut sauce, 89
cellophane noodles in hot sauce with broccoli, 120–1
fried noodles with broccoli, 115–16
buns, steamed filled (bao), 45–6

cabbage, Chinese, 29, 30
Chinese greens and coriander soup, 51
Chinese greens with peanut dressing, 74–5

noodle and Chinese cabbage soup, 50
quick fried cabbage with eggs, 131
carrots: carrot and apple salad, 71–2
norimaki sushi, 107–9
orange and white vinegared salad, 75–6
cashew nuts: crisp sweet cashews, 43
foo yong eggs and cashew nuts, 133
casserole noodles with floating eggs, 124
celery and green pepper with sesame sauce, 36
cellophane noodles *see* noodles
chakin sushi, 34–6
chestnut rice, 97
chillies, 18–19
chilli flowers, 111
pickled chilli peppers, 62
Chinese almond biscuits, 143
Chinese egg drop soup, 51–2
Chinese egg rolls, 40–1
Chinese eggs and tomatoes, 132
Chinese fried rice with mixed vegetables, 102-3
Chinese greens, 29–30
Chinese greens with peanut dressing, 74–5
Chinese leaves, 29
Chinese pancakes, 116
Chinese pickled ginger, 66–7
Chinese steamed omelette, 129–30
Chinese Szechwan preserved vegetables, 19
Chinese tea eggs, 133
Chinese vegetables in sauce with plain soft fried noodles, 122–3
chira sushi, 106–7
chrysanthemum turnips, 85
clear soup with lemon and beancurd, 58
coconut: broccoli with lemon and coconut sauce, 89
coconut filled pancakes, 144–5
grapefruit and coconut salad, 69–70
green salad with coconut sauce, 88
mixed vegetable salad with coconut sauce, 87–8
pan roasted coconut with peanuts, 44
coconut cream, 21–2
coconut milk, 19–22
baked coconut custard, 147–8
coconut batter pancakes, 145
cooked vegetable salad in coconut sauce, 67–8
lemon, beancurd and coconut milk soup, 52
sweet smelling coconut rice, 98
yellow rice with coconut milk, 97
combination fried rice, 104–5
coriander, 22
Chinese greens and coriander soup, 51
mushroom and coriander soup, 50–1
corn fritters, 43–4
cos lettuce in cream sauce, 82–3
crackling bananas, 148
cream sauce, cos lettuce in, 82–3
crisp sweet walnuts or cashews, 43
cucumber: beansprout and cucumber salad, 74
cucumber and mushrooms, 85
cucumber and wakame salad, 73
cucumber relish, 62
cucumber salad, 70–1
mild fresh Chinese pickled cucumber, 67
norimaki sushi, 108–9
spicy lemon cucumber salad, 34
Vik's Viking cucumber pickle, 64–5
cumin, 22–3
curries: beancurd and vegetable, 138–9
Thai fried curried rice, 103
curry leaves, 23
custard: almond custard in orange-flower syrup, 149
baked coconut custard, 147–8

daikon *see* radish, white
daun salem leaves, 23
desserts, 141–50
dipping sauces, 136
donburi: tempura, 109
  vegetable, 109
dressings, 59, 61, 77–8
  beancurd, 77
  Japanese mustard, 76, 77
  Japanese white, 77–8
  sesame seed and soya, 75, 78
dumplings, rice flour, 55–6

egg noodles in vegetable stock, 115
egg rolls, Chinese, 40–1
eggs, 127–33
  casserole noodles with floating eggs, 124
  cellophane noodles, egg and vegetables, 119–20
  chakin sushi, 34–6
  Chinese egg drop soup, 51–2
  Chinese eggs and tomatoes, 132
  Chinese steamed omelette, 129–30
  Chinese tea eggs, 133
  eggs on a vegetable nest, 128–9
  foo yong eggs and cashew nuts, 133
  hardboiled eggs with hot sauce, 130
  norimaki sushi, 108–9
  plump horses, 39
  quick fried cabbage with eggs, 131
  son-in-law eggs, 38
  soya eggs with plum sauce, 130–1
  spinach rolled omelette, 128
equipment, 16

festive rice cone, 110–11
festive rice pudding, 149–50
foo yong eggs and cashew nuts, 133
four fruits soup, 56
French beans: norimaki sushi, 108–9
fried ball cake, 147

fritters, corn, 43–4
fruit: fruit tempura with honey, 142–3
  Indonesian fruit salad, 71
  toffee fruit, 143

galloping horses, 40
garlic, fried peanuts with onion and, 42–3
ginger, 24
  baked ginger and citrus bananas, 146
  Chinese pickled ginger, 66–7
  ginger and mushroom soup, 54–5
  preserved red ginger, 66
  spinach and ginger soup, 52–3
grapefruit and coconut salad, 69–70
grapes: apples and grapes with Japanese mustard dressing, 76
green beans, 83
  bamboo shoot and green bean soup, 53–4
  green beans with sesame and sherry sauce, 83
  spiced stir fried green beans, 84
green rice, 96
green salad with coconut sauce, 88

hardboiled eggs with hot sauce, 130
honey: fruit tempura with, 142–3
  honey glazed mushrooms, 92
hot green vegetable rice, 110
hot sauce, 120–1, 130, 140
Hunan vegetable hotpot, 88

Indonesian fruit salad, 71

Japanese egg noodles with side salad, 125–6
Japanese fried rice, 101–2
Japanese mustard dressing, 76, 77
Japanese noodles, 121–2
Japanese pancakes, 131–2
Japanese quick pickles, 63–4
Japanese skewered vegetables, 86–7
Japanese stock, 50
Japanese white dressing, 77–8

kebabs: Japanese skewered vegetables, 86–7
kecap, 24

laos, 24
lemon: broccoli with lemon and coconut sauce, 89
  clear soup with lemon and beancurd, 58
  lemon, beancurd and coconut milk soup, 52
  mushroom and vegetable salad in lemon shells, 37–8
  spicy lemon cucumber salad, 34
lemon grass, 24
lettuce in cream sauce, 82–3
light-jewel pudding, 149–50
loh baak *see* radish, white
lotus roots, 30
  norimaki sushi, 107–9
lotus seed bao, 45

mangoes, sticky rice with, 145–6
mee krob, 118–19
melon, pickled, 64
mirin, 25
miso, 25
  chilled summer vegetable miso soup, 57
  miso and vegetable soup, 57
mushrooms: cucumber and mushrooms, 85
  honey glazed mushrooms, 92
  mushroom and coriander soup, 50–1
  mushroom and vegetable salad in lemon shells, 37–8
  norimaki sushi, 108–9
  plump horses, 39
mushrooms, Chinese dried black, 23
  ginger and mushroom soup, 54–5
  mushrooms and rice, 99–100
  stuffed Chinese mushrooms with sherry sauce, 37
mustard: Japanese mustard dressing, 76, 77
  Vik's Viking mustard mixed pickle, 65

nasi gemuk, 99
nigiri sushi, 106
noodles, 112–26
  braised noodles, 116
  casserole noodles with floating eggs, 124
  cellophane noodles, egg and vegetables, 119–20
  cellophane noodles in hot sauce with broccoli, 120–1
  Chinese vegetables in sauce with plain soft fried noodles, 122–3
  deep fried noodle wrapped water chestnuts, 33–4
  deep fried noodles (yaki soba), 124–5
  egg noodles in vegetable stock, 115
  fried noodles with broccoli, 115–16
  Japanese, 121–2
  Japanese egg noodles with side salad, 125–6
  noodle and Chinese cabbage soup, 50
  noodles with combination topping, 117–18
  soba (buckwheat flour noodles), 121–2
  summer noodles, 125
  Thai crisp noodles, 118–19
  Thai fried noodles, 117
  udon or soba in soup stock, 122
  udon (wheat flour noodles), 121–2
nori, 25
norimaki sushi, 107–9

oden, 86
omelettes: chakin sushi, 34–6
  Chinese steamed, 129–30
  spinach rolled, 128
onions, 26
  braised aubergines with peppers and onions, 89–90
  fried peanuts with garlic and onion, 42–3
orange and white vinegared salad, 75–6

orange-flower syrup, almond custard in, 149
oven temperatures, 152

pancakes: banana, 144
   Chinese, 116
   coconut batter, 145
   coconut filled, 144–5
   Japanese, 131–2
peanut butter: Chinese greens with peanut dressing, 74–5
peanuts, 26
   dry roasted peanuts, 41–2
   fried peanuts, 42
   fried peanuts with garlic and onion, 42–3
   pan roasted coconut with peanuts, 44
pears, crackling 148
peppers: braised aubergines with peppers and onions, 89–90
   celery and green pepper with sesame sauce, 36
pickles, 59–67
   Chinese pickled ginger, 66–7
   cucumber relish, 62
   Japanese quick pickles, 63–4
   mild fresh Chinese pickled cucumber, 67
   mixed vegetable (salt pressed) pickle, 63
   mixed vegetable (vinegar pressed) pickle, 63
   pickled chilli peppers, 62
   pickled melon, 64
   preserved red ginger, 66
   sweet white radish or turnip pickle, 64
   Szechwan pickled vegetables, 65–6
   Thai pickled mixed vegetables, 61–2
   Vik's Viking cucumber pickle, 64–5
   Vik's Viking mustard mixed pickle, 65
pineapple: galloping horses, 40
   rice stuffed pineapple, 101
plum sauce, soya eggs with, 130–1
plump horses, 39
preserved red ginger, 66

radish, white (daikon), 23, 30–1
   mushroom and vegetable salad in lemon shells, 37–8
   orange and white vinegared salad, 75–6
   sweet white radish pickle, 64
red rice, 95–6
relish, cucumber, 62
rice, 93–111
   beancurd and broccoli fried rice, 103–4
   chakin sushi, 34–6
   chestnut rice, 97
   Chinese fried rice with mixed vegetables, 102–3
   chira sushi, 106–7
   combination fried rice, 104–5
   festive rice cone, 110–11
   festive rice pudding, 149–50
   fried rice, 100–5
   galloping horses, 40
   green rice, 96
   hot green vegetable rice, 110
   Japanese fried rice, 101–2
   mushrooms and rice, 99–100
   nigiri sushi, 106
   norimaki sushi, 107–9
   plain boiled rice, 95
   red rice, 95–6
   rice and beansprouts, 100
   rice stuffed pineapple, 101
   spiced rice, 99
   sticky rice with mangoes, 145–6
   sushi rice dishes, 105–9
   sweet smelling coconut rice, 98
   tempura donburi, 109
   Thai fried curried rice, 103
   Thai fried rice, 101
   thick rice soup, 56
   vegetable donburi, 109
   yellow rice with coconut milk, 97
   yellow rice with spices, 98
rice flour dumplings, 55–6

salads, 59–61, 67–76

apples and grapes with Japanese mustard dressing, 76
beansprout and cucumber, 74
carrot and apple, 71–2
Chinese greens with peanut dressing, 74–5
cooked vegetable salad in coconut sauce, 67–8
cucumber, 70–1
cucumber and wakame, 73
fried aubergine, 73
grapefruit and coconut, 69–70
green salad with coconut sauce, 88
Indonesian fruit salad, 71
Japanese egg noodles with side salad, 125–6
mixed vegetable salad with coconut sauce, 87–8
mixed-up beansprout, 74
mushroom and vegetable salad in lemon shells, 37–8
orange and white vinegared, 75–6
spicy lemon cucumber, 34
spinach, 72–3
spinach with sesame seed and soya dressing, 75
sweet and sour vegetable and beancurd, 137
vegetable salad with hot sauce, 68–9
white, 72
sambal, 26
santan *see* coconut milk
sauces: coconut, 87–8
cream, 82–3
dipping, 136
hot, 120–1, 130, 140
lemon and coconut, 89
sesame and sherry, 83
seasoned and fried tempe, 140
serundeng, 44
sesame paste, 26
sesame seeds, 26
celery and green pepper with sesame sauce, 36
green beans with sesame and sherry sauce, 83
sesame seed and soya dressing, 75, 78
walnut sesame bao, 45–6
shallow fried bananas, 146
shark's fin soup, vegetarian, 54
sherry: green beans with sesame and sherry sauce, 83
stuffed Chinese mushrooms with sherry sauce, 37
shiitake, 23–4
mushrooms and rice, 99–100
shoyu, 27
snow fungus, 27
soba (buckwheat flour noodles), 27, 121–2
somen, 27
son-in-law eggs, 38
soups, 47, 50–8
bamboo shoot and green bean, 53–4
chilled summer vegetable miso, 57
Chinese egg drop, 51–2
Chinese greens and coriander, 51
clear soup with lemon and beancurd, 58
four fruits, 56
ginger and mushroom, 54–5
lemon, beancurd and coconut milk, 52
miso and vegetable, 57
mushroom and coriander, 50–1
noodle and Chinese cabbage, 50
spinach and ginger, 52–3
thick rice, 56
vegetable soup with rice flour dumplings, 55–6
vegetarian shark's fin, 54
watercress, 57–8
soya sauce, 27–8
aubergines and tomatoes cooked with, 81–2
sesame seed and soya dressing, 75, 78
soya eggs with plum sauce, 130–1
spiced rice, 99
spiced stir fried green beans, 84
spicy aubergines, 81

spicy lemon cucumber salad, 34
spinach: green rice, 96
   norimaki sushi, 108–9
   spinach and ginger soup, 52–3
   spinach rolled omelette, 128
   spinach salad, 72–3
   spinach salad with sesame seed and soya dressing, 75
starters, 32–46
sticky rice with mangoes, 145–6
stocks, 47–50
   Japanese, 50
   Thai, 49
   vegetable, 48–50
summer noodles, 125
sushi rice dishes, 105–9
   chakin sushi, 34–6
sweet and sour vegetable and beancurd salad, 137
sweet smelling coconut rice, 98
sweetcorn fritters, 43–4
Szechwan pepper, 28
Szechwan pickled vegetables, 65–6

tahu *see* beancurd
tamarind, 28
tea eggs, Chinese, 133
tempe, 17
   fried tempe, 139–40
   fried tempe in hot sauce, 140
   seasoned and fried tempe, 140
tempura: fruit with honey, 142–3
   tempura donburi, 109
Thai crisp noodles, 118–19
Thai curried beancurd with vegetables, 90
Thai fried curried rice, 103
Thai fried noodles, 117
Thai fried rice, 101
Thai pickled mixed vegetables, 61–2
Thai stock, 49
toffee fruit, 143
tofu *see* beancurd
togarashi, 29
tomato: aubergines and tomatoes cooked with soya sauce, 81–2
   Chinese eggs and tomatoes, 132
turnips: chrysanthemum turnips, 85

sweet turnip pickle, 64

udon (wheat flour noodles), 121–2
urap, 87

vegetable stock, egg noodles in, 115
vegetables, 29–31, 79–92
   beancurd and vegetable curry, 138–9
   cellophane noodles, egg and vegetables, 119–20
   chilled summer vegetable miso soup, 57
   Chinese fried rice with mixed vegetables, 102–3
   Chinese vegetables in sauce with plain soft fried noodles, 122–3
   eggs on a vegetable nest, 128–9
   hot green vegetable rice, 110
   Hunan vegetable hotpot, 88
   Japanese quick pickles, 63–4
   Japanese skewered vegetables, 86–7
   miso and vegetable soup, 57
   mixed vegetable salad with coconut sauce, 87–8
   mixed vegetables and beancurd, 138
   oden, 86
   stir fried vegetables, 90–1
   Szechwan pickled vegetables, 65–6
   Thai curried beancurd with vegetables, 90
   Thai pickled mixed vegetables, 61–2
   vegetable bao, 46
   vegetable donburi, 109
   vegetable soup with rice flour dumplings, 55–6
   vegetable stocks, 48–50
   yellow and green summer vegetables, 91–2
   see also salads *and individual types of vegetable*
vegetarian shark's fin soup, 54
Vik's Viking cucumber pickle, 64–5

Vik's Viking mustard mixed pickle, 65
vinegar, 31

wakame and cucumber salad, 73
walnuts: crisp sweet walnuts, 43
    walnut sesame bao, 45–6
wasabi, 31
water chestnuts, 30
    deep fried noodle wrapped water chestnuts, 33–4
watercress: norimaki sushi, 108–9
    stir fried watercress, 84
    watercress soup, 57–8
weights and measures, 151–2
white salad, 72
won-tun, fried, 114

yaki soba, 124–5
yellow and green summer vegetables, 91–2
yellow rice with coconut milk, 97
yellow rice with spices, 98